FREUD

FREUD

O. MANNONI

Translated from the French by Renaud Bruce

PANTHEON BOOKS

A DIVISION OF RANDOM HOUSE · NEW YORK

Library of Congress Catalog Card Number: 73-123726

ISBN: 0-394-42560-X

Manufactured in the United States of America
by The Book Press

2 4 6 8 9 7 5 3

First American Edition

AUTHOR'S NOTE
TO THIS TRANSLATION

WHEN A FRENCH PUBLISHING HOUSE ASKED ME TO WRITE a study of Freud for one of its very strictly limited series (170 pages of 400 words each), the task at first seemed impossible to me.

However, in accepting the challenge I was to discover its benefits: such rigorous limits forced me to emphasize the essential elements more sharply than I would have done if there had been no restrictions.

Nor have I taken advantage of this English translation to make any changes in the fast-paced, concise style I used, or in the perspective I had felt obliged to select, which put the originality of psychoanalysis in its earliest stages in the foreground and provided only a glimpse, as if from a great distance, of the modifications and contributions revealed in Freud's later work. Too often the opposite perspective has been chosen.

I have, nonetheless, added a few lines in those areas where sacrifices had been too exacting, and at the request of Pantheon I have added an afterword which quickly traces the destiny of psychoanalysis after Freud.

CONTENTS

ILLUSTRATIONS

(between pages 118 and 119)

FREUD

CHAPTER ONE

"My Life Is of No Interest
Except in Its Relation to Psychoanalysis . . ."

ALTHOUGH IT HAS RE-
markable literary qualities, Freud's work does not belong
primarily to literature: it aims toward a truth. Commentators on such a work have to choose between several approaches, according to their own vision of truth.

The Freudian doctrine remains open to interpretations, to new developments, and to corrections, but that
kind of work will not concern us here. What we will
focus on is the truth of Freud himself—the way in which
he arrived at the questions he posed and then at the answers he gave. As far as that is possible, the task consists
in giving an idea of the work as it was created and in
showing Freud doing it, without pretending to follow
him step by step while not anticipating the future, for
most often what comes later clarifies difficulties that were
seen only dimly at first and permits us to describe them
correctly.

To biographers, it may have seemed that something
in his past had prepared Freud for his discoveries, but
equally, that chance encounters led him to them. If he

had been more successful with his histological slides, if Bertha Pappenheim had not been his fiancée's friend, if his professors had refused him the travel grant . . . So many "ifs" emphasize the contingencies of his career and spare us the task of searching in it for the kind of mystical predestination attributed to heroes. But there is no doubt that once he was engaged, however tentatively, in a dialogue with hysteria, he went his own way, far from all clearly marked paths, without letting himself be diverted by anything—especially opposition. It is not easy, therefore, to fix a career such as Freud's in exact historical context. From the medical milieu of Vienna at that time, with its aspirations, its contradictions, and even its dreams, one could infer the probable circumstances of a poor Jewish physician who is passionately devoted to research and awaits some success which will bring him renown and position. But one could not infer that he would enter into violent conflict with that milieu because of his discovery of the unconscious. Today Freud's discovery is a part of what we call modernity, but when it emerged there was nothing "modern" about it. Freud could even write, speaking of himself: "The author of *The Interpretation of Dreams* has ventured, in the face of the reproaches of strict science, to become a partisan of antiquity and superstition."[1] That it went counter to contemporary beliefs is part of the essence of psychoanalysis, and in spite of appearances, that is still true. The recently published book on Woodrow Wilson* provoked similar opposition.

If psychoanalysis has antecedents—and evidently it has—they were not recognized as such until they were

---

* Sigmund Freud and William C. Bullitt, *Thomas Woodrow Wilson, Twenty-eighth President of the United States* (Boston, Houghton Mifflin Company, 1967).

brought to light retrospectively, as it were, by psycho-analysis itself. Ludwig Börne, for example, had a profound influence on Freud, who read him when he was fourteen, but it is Freud who made it possible for Börne to be regarded today as more than a minor political symbol. And when the influences which made an imprint on Freud are assembled, they form a chaos awaiting an act of creation . . . The questions posed by Freud were ones that his age did not think of asking—or, if they were asked, the age did not want to hear anything about them. In other words, Freud made history rather than being made by it, and therefore his position is the opposite of that of the followers of modernity.

Psychoanalysis and Biography

It is well known that Freud never abandoned or denied a single one of his ideas when he went beyond it. His life and the development of his thought constitute a continuous *Aufhebung*—a suppressing and conserving. He not only preserved—by going beyond them—Breuer's catharsis and the trauma of his first etiological hypotheses, but it can be said that he did the same for the beliefs and superstitions of the most remote past. But that presumes a special ability to erase. For example, eighteen days before his twenty-ninth birthday he burned all his papers. Later, he would do the same periodically. On that particular occasion, in 1885, he wanted to mark in this way "the great turning point in his life." And indeed it was the great turning point, though he did not know it. He always believed that it was his marriage and giving up research!

Here is how he presented things to his fiancée Martha in a letter dated April 28, 1885:

One intention as a matter of fact I have almost finished carrying out, an intention which a number of as yet unborn and unfortunate people will one day resent. Since you won't guess what kind of people I am referring to, I will tell you at once: they are my biographers. I have destroyed all my notes of the past fourteen years, as well as letters, scientific excerpts, and the manuscripts of my papers . . . all my thoughts and feelings about the world in general and about myself in particular have been found unworthy of further existence. They will now have to be thought all over again, and I certainly had accumulated some scribbling. . . . As for the biographers, let them worry, we have no desire to make it too easy for them. Each one of them will be right in his opinion of "The Development of the Hero."[2]

We see every day how writers erase (*all my thoughts and feelings . . . will now have to be thought all over again*) and how critics or biographers strive to read what has been erased. These are two opposite ways of *conserving*. Few people have been as faithful to their past as Freud, even those who have piously kept even the least important document pertaining to it. But he had always been suspicious of the curiosity of biographers, and had even doubted the feasibility of their task. In a letter dated May 18, 1936, he remarked: "Anyone turning biographer commits himself to lies, to concealment, to hypocrisy, to flattery, and even to hiding his own lack of understanding, for biographical truth is not to be had, and even if it were it couldn't be used."[3]

In any case, the relationship between analytic technique and the art of biography is an ambiguous one. They resemble each other, they appear to be designed to help each other, but there is between them an ineradicable opposition. A biographer who is not an analyst may note that we are rather ill-informed about Freud's personal life; he may hope, and we may hope with him, that it was more varied and fuller than what we can glimpse behind Freud's scientific life. He can also become impatient waiting for so many letters that are still in private hands. But if Freud's biographies are generally rather deceptive, it is not so much because the biographer wanted to confine himself to hypocritical hagiography or to conceal scandalous secrets; it is because a biography, as far as Freud is concerned, cannot be written by omitting the perspective of analytic *truth*, which renders superficial and banal that perspective of *reality* outside of which biography cannot deploy its art. In fact, the confidences about his youth that Freud has imparted to us are in the nature of by-products of his scientific discoveries. It is easy to give an example of this. In a letter to Wilhelm Fliess dated October 3, 1897, which he could write without thinking of his biographers, Freud, in giving an account of the progress of his own analysis, provides one of those facts that a biographer can only carefully gather: "I welcomed my one-year-younger brother (who died within a few months) with ill wishes and real infantile jealousy, and . . . his death left the germ of guilt in me."[4] The remarkable thing that happened here to Freud is not that between the ages of one and two he had feelings of jealousy toward a younger brother, that being the case for so many children, but rather that the memory of it should have come to him at the age of forty-one, right at the time when he was beginning to gain insight into his Oedipus complex (something which had never yet been realized by anyone, not even Sophocles, naturally) and had suddenly become capable of understanding his childhood memories. Thus his biography

acquires meaning only in relation to psychoanalysis.
When Freud himself wrote, "My life is of no interest
except in its relation to psychoanalysis," it was neither a
banality nor an evasion. Illusion, belief in the "myth of
the hero," our own resistances, lead us to believe that if
we knew the details of Freud's childhood better, certain
obscurities—which ones?—would be cleared away. Yet
like him, thanks to him, and in any case following him,
we would end by finding in them the very bases of
analysis—beginning with the Oedipus complex—as they
are found in everyone and in one's own self. The patient
in analysis does not bend over his past like an old man
writing his memoirs. He is less occupied with restoring
his past than with going beyond it, which is the only real
way of preserving it.

Memories

Among the memories which, like models, accompanied
the progress of his own analysis, there were some that he
did not want to expose as being his and which he attributed to some imaginary person. That is how we know
what was for him the lost paradise and the regret which
is part of unconscious desire:

> I was the child of people who were originally well-
> to-do and who, I fancy, lived comfortably enough in
> that little corner of the provinces. When I was about
> three, the branch of industry in which my father was
> concerned met with a catastrophe. He lost all his
> means and we were forced to leave the place and
> move to a large town. Long and difficult years fol-
> lowed, of which, as it seems to me, nothing was
> worth remembering. I never felt really comfortable

in the town. I believe now that I was never free from a longing for the beautiful woods near our home, in which (as one of my memories from those days tells me) I used to run off from my father, almost before I had learnt to walk.[5]

Freud never stopped detesting Vienna, without consenting to leave it; it was there that he had suffered and endured humiliation, and it seemed to him it was only there that he ought to take his revenge. He had truly suffered there—first of all from great poverty. The hope, not to become rich, but to find security was always present in his preoccupations. In his imagination he was pursued by the specter of poverty and hunger, even when he no longer had anything to fear from it in actuality.

Vocation

In this same 1899 paper, Freud tells of a vacation visit to his native Moravia, and describes his state of mind upon entering the University twenty-six years earlier:

I was seventeen, and in the family where I was staying there was a daughter of fifteen, with whom I immediately fell in love. It was my first calf-love and sufficiently intense, but I kept it completely secret. After a few days the girl went off to her school (from which she too was home for the holidays) and it was this separation after such a short acquaintance that brought my longings to a really high pitch. I passed many hours in solitary walks through the lovely woods that I had found once more and spent my time building castles in the air. These, strangely enough, were not concerned with the future but

9

sought to improve the past. If only the smash had not occurred! If only I had stopped at home and grown up in the country and grown as strong as the young men in the house, the brothers of my love! And then if only I had followed my father's profession and if I had finally married her—for I should have known her intimately all those years! I had not the slightest doubt, of course, that in the circumstances created by my imagination I should have loved her just as passionately as I really seemed to then.[6]

The young girl's name was Gisela Fluss. Some thirty years later, while taking notes after a day's work on the case of the "Rat Man," Freud made a *lapsus calami*. His patient had talked about a Gisela, and Freud wrote it down as "Gisela Fluss." He contented himself with putting an exclamation point beside it—intended only for his own eyes.

These nostalgic reveries which turned toward the past were accompanied by some difficulty in envisaging the future. In 1875, with two years of medical studies already behind him, Freud visited his half-brother Philipp and half-niece Pauline in Manchester. His purpose was to see if he could rediscover a profession like his father's, with cotton replacing wool and Pauline replacing Gisela. But Pauline was not Gisela.

Freud always resigned himself rather reluctantly to medical studies. Nevertheless that wrong choice made for the wrong reasons led him, thanks to a very poor nomenclature (that of "nervous" illnesses), not to his true vocation, which probably does not mean anything, but to a vocation out of which he created what we know.

At the University, he missed his secondary-school studies. He had been a very good student at the Sperl

Gymnasium and his years there remained a fond memory. His acquaintance with history and the humanities, acquired at the Sperl, "in my case was to bring me as much consolation as anything else in the struggles of life." As for his first contacts with the sciences, he said later, with an irony he was able to permit himself in retrospect, that it seemed he had merely to select the one to which he would bring abilities that would prove invaluable. He seemed to remember that "through the whole of this time there ran a premonition of a task ahead, till it found open expression in my school-leaving essay as a wish that I might during the course of my life contribute something to our human knowledge."[7]

The subject of that essay was "What must be considered in the choice of a profession?" Unfortunately—or fortunately—the juvenilia of great men are not always found. But we do have a letter, the oldest of Freud's letters in our possession, written to a childhood friend, Emil Fluss, where he mentions that essay:

> Incidentally, my professor told me—and he is the first person who has dared to tell me this—that I possess what Herder so nicely calls an *idiotic* style—i.e., a style at once correct and characteristic. . . . You . . . until now have probably remained unaware that you have been exchanging letters with a German stylist. And now I advise you as a friend, not as an interested party, to preserve them—have them bound—take good care of them—one never knows.[8]

The advice was good, as had been the appreciation of the examiner: Freud is a stylist to whom a translation does not do justice. But that playful schoolboy had very serious, almost tragic preoccupations:

You take my "worries about the future" too lightly. People who fear nothing but mediocrity, you say, are safe. Safe from what? I ask. Surely not safe and secure from being mediocre? . . . Admittedly more powerful intellects are also seized with doubts about themselves; does it therefore follow that anyone who doubts his virtues is of powerful intellect? . . . The magnificence of the world rests after all on this wealth of possibilities, except that it is unfortunately not a firm basis for self-knowledge.[9]

There is nothing prophetic in that rhetoric. The seventeen-year-old Freud speaks as a humanist or moralist. His lucidity, his pessimism, his distrust of illusions, his proclivity for serious thought—all that fits into the most venerable forms of wisdom, and does not even distantly forecast anything resembling analytic curiosity.

Here is how his situation could be summed up: The romantic expectation that the future will return to me what has been lost must give way to realism and wisdom. But is there some road in life whose goal is wisdom? At the Sperl Gymnasium, Freud had been able to believe there was. He would later write:

Neither at that time, nor indeed in my later life, did I feel any particular predilection for the career of a doctor. I was moved, rather, by a sort of curiosity, which was, however, directed more towards human concerns than towards natural objects; nor had I grasped the importance of observation as one of the best means of gratifying it. . . . Under the powerful influence of a school friendship with a boy rather my senior who grew up to be a well-known politician, I developed a wish to study law like him and to engage in social activities. [The question was

whether or not to be active in a party of social opposition.] At the same time, the theories of Darwin,
which were then of topical interest, strongly attracted me, for they held out hopes of an extraordinary advance in our understanding of the world;
and it was hearing Goethe's beautiful essay on Nature [attributed to Goethe] read aloud at a popular
lecture by Professor Carl Brühl just before I left
school that decided me to become a medical student.[10]

Freud was to retain something of his political day-
dreams and of his need to participate actively in some
kind of opposition. He saw psychoanalysis as a "movement," and the societies he founded displayed that character, even if this is no longer evident in their present
form. On the other hand, Darwin and Goethe contributed rather wrong-headed and even contradictory reasons
for his choice of profession, since the essay he attributes to
Goethe in the letter just cited represents Nature as a
woman who lets her children explore her secrets. One
might almost dare say that would be the more "analytic"
of the two! Freud was not loath to search for the secrets
of Nature. In Ernst Brücke's laboratory he proved that
the discipline of pure science suited him and all his life he
demonstrated that his relationship to patients interested
him. Yet there was something in medicine which he found
uncongenial. He would later put it into a sentence—
which, by the way, is self-contradictory: "After forty
years of medical practice, I know myself well enough to
know that I have never been a physician in the proper
sense of the word."

In spite of the fact that he delayed the completion of
his medical studies and tried to orient himself toward
teaching physiology, his detested poverty, his projected

marriage (to a poor girl) obliged him to resign himself. In 1882, he took for three years a position at the Vienna General Hospital.

It was at this time that Breuer made him privy to the treatment of Anna O., which had just been interrupted. Freud was interested, but he did not imagine that here was a means of avoiding medical practice. First, it would be necessary for Charcot to give scientific and medical dignity to the study of hysteria. For Freud was in fact searching for a complicated compromise: to escape medical practice, to oppose the views of the period, but finally to be recognized by the world of science and medicine. We know that he did not easily succeed.

Freud the Neurologist

Thus, Freud's career was established on a play on words: a *neurologist*, he had to treat *nervous* afflictions . . . But it was not yet so in the beginning, and besides, he had become a neurologist through his laboratory work. An initial research attempt to identify the male eel's sex glands, about which nothing was known, had been entrusted to him and he had successfully completed it. Brücke had given him another assignment—on the nervous system of the lamprey larva—and this was the subject of his first publication. He was now a neurologist. He published some twenty articles on neurology between 1877 and 1897. Twenty years! That the study of neurology could serve as preparation for psychology, as might naïvely have been believed, Freud himself would later formally deny. The cases of Breuer and Bernheim demonstrated that a general practitioner was in a better position than a neurologist to approach "nervous illnesses." Charcot represented the remarkable exception that was to change everything. Freud's book *On Aphasia* (1891) and his essay "Project for a Scientific Psychology" (1895) are among the remaining testimonials to the vain efforts made at that time to build a bridge between neurology and psychology. It is true that through some sort of materialistic act of faith, Freud did not abandon the hope that one day the two disciplines would join each other. But after 1895, he never again tried in a practical way to bring them into harmony.

When he had to leave the laboratory to establish a private practice, what was he going to do with a training which at that time basically consisted in the verification of diagnoses by autopsy? Nothnagel, a professor of neurology, had told Freud: "I suggest you go on working as before, but the papers you have done up to now won't be of any use to you; general practitioners, on whom everything depends, are prosaic people who will think to themselves: 'What's the good of Freud's knowledge of brain anatomy? That won't help him to treat a radialis paralysis!' "[11] But Freud knew only neurology; and it was as a neurologist that he was going to try to build his private practice.

Martha

Freud had wanted to marry Martha for a long time. He had been willing to postpone the marriage until better days, but he now decided that "the great turning point in his life" had come. We know only a very small part of Freud's correspondence with Martha Bernays, but that is filled with passion. The most classic fantasies of what

would be called some years later "engagement neurosis"
(an expression no longer in use), unjustified jealousy,
ideas of death, a whole symptomatology which would
later be food for Freud's thought, are found in it. That
marriage of two poor fiancés was nevertheless a bourgeois marriage, and money problems (the absence of
money) played a large role in it. The lack of security
and the risks to be taken almost made the marriage a
challenge to fate and gave it a romantic cast, but the
ideal pursued was a "reasonable" one. Freud counted
on moral strength and self-confidence to surmount material difficulties.

It seems that Martha kept her composure better
than Sigmund, who suffered from symptoms he would
not be able to explain until much later. On June 27,
1882, he wrote to Martha:

Yesterday I went to see my friend, Ernst v. Fleischl,
whom hitherto, so long as I did not know Marty
[i.e., Martha; curiously, he often spoke to her in
the third person], I envied in every respect. . . . he
has always been my ideal, and I was not satisfied
until we became friends and I could properly enjoy
his value and abilities. . . . it occurred to me how
much he could do for a girl like Martha, what a
setting he could provide for this jewel . . . how she
would enjoy sharing the importance and influence
of this lover, how the nine years which this man has
over me could mean as many unparalleled happy
years of her life compared to the nine miserable
years spent in hiding and near-helplessness that await
her with me. . . . And I began wondering what he
would think of Martha. Then all of a sudden I broke
off this daydream; . . . Can't I too for once have

something better than I deserve? Martha remains mine.[12]

There is no question of psychoanalyzing Freud; he took care of that himself. But is it surprising that someone capable of expressing such feelings should be the first to unravel the labyrinthine ways and complexities of jealousy (who loves whom)?

Two years later, in a letter dated March 29, 1884, he anticipated what was to be a real difficulty:

Heavens above, little woman, how innocent and good-natured you are! Don't you realize that this very science could become our bitterest enemy, that the irresistible temptation to devote one's life without remuneration or recognition to the solving of problems unconnected with our personal situation, could postpone or even destroy our chances of sharing life —if I, yes, if I were to go and lose my head over it? Now, this is out of the question; I feel in fine fettle and intend to exploit science rather than allow myself to be exploited in its favor.[13]

This letter was composed like the preceding one: (1) What would happen if . . . ? (2) But I choose what is sensible . . .

Events were to confirm the fact that Freud had chosen a wife according to his wishes. For many years, Martha—whom the whole family, Sigmund included, was to call "Mama"—was the recipient of love and respect from everyone. But this ideal marriage conformed to the traditions of Vienna's bourgeois circles, and in that area Freud was not an innovator. He had no interest whatever in the feminist movement, which was just beginning

17

to emerge at the time. In the John Stuart Mill essay on the emancipation of women that he translated, he saw only a utopian dream. The comparison of the feminine condition to that of slaves shocked him; he accused Mill of not having realized that humanity is divided between men and women. On this subject, as on some others (painting, for example), this revolutionary, who contributed more effectively than most—Mill included—to the liberation of women, unquestionably held a conformist position which might appear reactionary from today's perspective. It is in his theory that he proved to be truly revolutionary. We can refer for instance, to the last pages of "Analysis Terminable and Interminable" (1938) to see with what "objectivity" he considered the effects of the castration complex in both men and women. But it was unavoidable that resistance would use facile arguments *ad hominem* to attack scientific concepts.

Wisdom

It is, however, somewhat surprising that it was Freud (in 1883, it's true) who, in criticizing John Stuart Mill, made the following comment:

> "He was perhaps the man of the century who best managed to free himself from the domination of customary prejudices. On the other hand—and that always goes together with it—he lacked in many matters the sense of the absurd. . . ."[14]

He would later recognize that the feeling of the absurd can be a means of defense in the service of prejudice, but in any case, that feeling would no longer make him retreat so easily. What is in question here is the (ambiguous) value of wisdom.

To guide himself through the difficulties of life, Freud undoubtedly counted at first on the most traditional forms of wisdom. This was not a question of ordinary social conformity; on the contrary, he measured that conformity against another society with which he was much more familiar and which he had sought in his readings. He had taught himself Spanish, in order to read Cervantes, at an age when one has to fight the tendency to juvenile presumption. But having already read the ancient and German classics, he had a keen sense of what he owed them. When he was in Paris, did he not go to the Père-Lachaise to visit the grave of Ludwig Börne (who had died in 1837)? Freud read the contemporary French novelists, but he has told us that his real masters were the English and Scottish writers. The reason can easily be guessed: they treat human destiny in a realistic way, but on a foundation of romantic traditions in which there is a confrontation between fate and the hero's pride, though with weapons less unequal than in ancient tragedy. Social situation, education, and the formation of the personality are part of destiny; the image of the world is neither a useless reflection nor a pleasant picture of reality, but offers points of reference for finding one's way. Freud was not an artist. He valued literary art for its dramatic and moral content, and if as an excellent stylist he knew how to appreciate its form, it was for the manner in which it expressed and developed its content. This is especially surprising since he was the first—in 1905—to formulate a correct theory on the determining role of form! Here again the traditionalism of his taste contradicts the revolutionary aspect of his theories.

Before discovering a wisdom's insufficiencies and

limitations when cultivated by these means, he had taken it far. This can be seen in a letter written in 1883, where he tells of the life and suicide of a colleague, Nathan Weiss. That story, too long to be quoted, too compact to be summarized, begins with the remark, "his life was as though composed by a writer of fiction" and ends on the same note: "Thus his death was like his life, cut to a pattern: he all but screams for the novelist [like Abel's blood toward God] to preserve him for human memory."[15] This dramatic account constitutes the first "case history" written by Freud, but nothing in it forecasts psychoanalysis. It is only that the same qualities will be found again intact in the histories of analytic cases.

If Freud had followed an academic career—for instance, if he had succeeded in becoming a teacher of physiology—he might have been confirmed in that form of wisdom. He would then only have brought once more to humanity and to himself a very venerable and ancient ideal. But he was soon to meet Charcot, who would make him see what all wisdom cannot attain. When he spoke about it later, a formula for initiation came to his mind: *Introite et hic dii sunt*—"Enter, for here too are gods." Nevertheless, the fund of wisdom previously acquired was not to be useless, and we know that later he considered the study of literature an essential part of the training program for analysts.

CHAPTER TWO

Introite et Hic Dii Sunt

In THE BEGINNING OF THE fall of 1885, it was as a neurologist that Freud presented himself at the Salpêtrière. He brought Charcot his nerve-tissue slides prepared with the silver-staining technique which he had invented and which had won Breuer's praise, but Charcot showed little interest in them. Seeing Charcot among hysterical patients, he remembered Breuer's account of Anna O. and spoke of it to Charcot. But neither pure anatomy nor pure psychology seemed to interest his interlocutor. Freud was perplexed and suspicious at first, but finally had the idea of proposing that he translate Charcot's books into German. His offer was accepted and everything settled; he was invited to Charcot's home and given interesting assignments. He quickly came to understand Charcot's attitude better and to feel a great admiration for him.

> Charcot, who is one of the greatest of physicians and a man whose common sense borders on genius, is simply wrecking all my aims and opinions. I some-

times come out of his lectures as from out of Notre
Dame, with an entirely new idea about perfection.
. . . Whether the seed will ever bear any fruit, I don't
know; but what I do know is that no other human
being has ever affected me in the same way.[16]

Charcot created and suppressed symptoms through
words, but it was not magic, for he showed that the phenomena of hysteria obeyed certain laws.

Many of Charcot's demonstrations began by provoking in me and in other visitors a sense of astonishment and an inclination to scepticism, which we tried
to justify by an appeal to one of the theories of the
day. He was always friendly and patient in dealing
with such doubts, but he was also most decided; it
was in one of these discussions that (speaking of
theory) he remarked, "*Ça n'empêche pas d'exister*"
[the remark was addressed to Freud], a *mot* which
left an indelible mark upon my mind.[17]

In effect, Charcot treated clinical observations as facts
and inferred neurological theories from them, in contrast
to German clinicians, who would use a physiological
theory to explain "morbid states." But above all, Charcot's
experiments were going to force Freud to conceive of
the possibility of thought "separate from consciousness."
It was possible to observe the somatic effect of thought

without the group of the other mental processes,
the ego, knowing about it or being able to intervene
to prevent it. If we had called to mind the familiar
psychological difference between sleep and waking,
the strangeness of our hypothesis might have seemed
less. No one should object that the theory of a split-

ting of consciousness as a solution to the riddle of hysteria is much too remote to impress an unbiassed and untrained observer. For, by pronouncing posses- sion by a demon to be the cause of hysterical phe- nomena, the Middle Ages in fact chose this solution; it would only have been a matter of exchanging the religious terminology of that dark and superstitious age for the scientific language of to-day.[18]

Nothing in this text must be construed as presaging the discovery of the unconscious. It was referring to something like the dual personality ascribed exclusively to hysterics, and not to the existence of unconscious "normal" thought.

There are signs that Freud, through the admiration he felt for Charcot, was identifying with a hysteric. This was an important point, which was later to influence the orientation of his research.

Up to that time Freud had suffered from various dis- orders which today would be called (although vaguely) "psychosomatic." He classified his affliction as "neuras- thenia," which was believed at the time to be physical and incurable. We see him worried about his heredity (he found it tainted) and the difficulties that life might still have in store for him: for Charcot, hysteria was "heredity plus *agents provocateurs.*" He writes Martha that he depends on her to save him from remaining sick (with "neurasthenia," he says). As Charcot did not treat hysterics, it would take some time for Freud to consider himself his own patient and diagnose himself as a hysteric (in letters to Fliess).

Almost at the same time, William James was also identifying with a patient. But in his case it was an epi- leptic in an asylum, and all James could learn from the

incident was that it involved "a variety of religious experience" urging him to have compassion on the unfortunate. Later, A. A. Brill saw himself as one of the schizophrenics he was treating in Zurich. But Freud's ideas
were known by then and Brill could be reassured that
"pathological mechanisms" exist in normal people also.
Freud, who furnished that loophole, did not yet have
it at his own disposal in 1885. He had to go the whole
way in order to escape from the traditional psychiatric
segregation, which labeled the patient "mad" and enclosed the physician within his impotent reason. Today,
analyst candidates are required to re-create that situation
by taking the role of the patient during the course of
their training analysis.

"He Was a Man of Brilliant Intellect"

When Freud opened his office in Vienna (Easter, 1886),
the cases that he took were neurological ones. Later, he
would write:

> My therapeutic arsenal contained only two weapons,
> electrotherapy and hypnotism [at the beginning,
> only one: electrotherapy], for prescribing a visit to
> a hydropathic establishment after a single consulta-
> tion was an inadequate source of income. My knowl-
> edge of electrotherapy was derived from W. Erb's
> text-book [1882], which provided detailed instruc-
> tions for the treatment of all the symptoms of nerv-
> ous diseases.[19]

He was compelled to see that those instructions were
useless, and that, he said, helped to rid him of the remnants of a naïve faith in authority.

So I put my electrical apparatus aside, even before
Moebius had saved the situation by explaining that
the successes of electric treatment in nervous disorders (in so far as there were any) were the effect
of suggestion on the part of the physician.[20]

One would like Freud to have discovered that effect of
"suggestion" himself. But on his return from Paris, he
was still searching for a neurological treatment and was
not interested in the psychological side of the cases he
was treating.

Hypnosis, however, gave results. Charcot used it,
but cared little about therapy. On the other hand, the
Nancy school (Bernheim, Liébeault) had been treating
with suggestion under hypnosis, and Freud was interested
in this. But above all, he had not forgotten that Breuer
had treated a case somewhat in this fashion. He asked
him to speak of it again. Breuer read him his notes, and,
after a great deal of resistance, finally agreed to collaborate with Freud on a book on hysteria. Apparently,
Breuer had conducted only one psychotherapy, that of
Anna O. But what he had done was highly original.
He had not used suggestion (which Freud had at first);
the patient's symptoms had disappeared when she herself found (under hypnosis) their origin and their explanation. Nothing, it seemed, had prepared Breuer for
this kind of therapy: he just let his patient proceed
on her own. She was an original, cultivated, imaginative
girl whom hysteria had paralyzed, literally and figura-
tively. We know her real name: Bertha Pappenheim. It
was she who directed the treatment.

The hypothesis, which seemed to Breuer to explain
the clinical facts, was that hysteria was characterized by
the retention of certain memories. As that retention resem-

bled posthypnotic amnesia, Breuer had given the name of "hypnoid states" to moments of consciousness, or to a "segment" of consciousness during which "ideas" did not associate but remained isolated, giving an impression of "hysterical retention." Behind each symptom one could suspect a memory thus "retained"; by being brought to consciousness the symptom was eliminated, and in this manner the symptoms could be treated, one by one.

Breuer called this method "cathartic," etymologically comparing it to a purgation, which is understandable in view of his concept of psychic retention. His patient compared it to chimney sweeping. The case of Bertha Pappenheim, which appears in the *Studies on Hysteria* under the name of Anna O., can still be read with much interest.

If only because it did not try to influence the patient but only attempted to have him find again what was his, the cathartic method is really at the origin of psychoanalysis. We can understand why Freud, at a time when he had fallen out with Breuer, could declare in a lecture at Clark University:

> If it is a merit to have brought psycho-analysis into being, that merit is not mine. I had no share in its earliest beginnings. I was a student . . . when another Viennese physician, Dr. Josef Breuer, first (in 1880–2) made use of this procedure on a girl who was suffering from hysteria.[21]

The matter is far less simple. The decisive character of Breuer's contribution has often been denied; but at other times it has been underestimated how simplistic the cathartic method really was compared with what psychoanalysis was to become. Let us consider the following points: (1) Breuer lost interest in the matter; we will see why in a moment. Freud was able to say, facetiously, that he must really have been the inventor, because it was he and not Breuer that the opponents took to task. (2) Then, Freud devised a theory other than that of retention and of "hypnoid states," and his theory was quickly shown to be more fruitful. (3) Then, and most importantly, Freud during his friendship with Fliess went through states of "transference" which completely changed his point of view. (4) Finally, catharsis was only a method of therapy for hysteria; nothing in it promised the possible emergence of a theoretical knowledge valid for all forms of thought, normal or not.

If Breuer lost interest in what he had himself discovered, it was because, for obscure countertransferential reasons (nothing was known about that at the time), he had felt a great deal of guilt when faced with sudden transference manifestations from his patient. He did not tell Freud the end of Anna O.'s story; but Freud in time was able to reconstruct it from partial confidences; he submitted the reconstruction to Breuer, who then admitted that it was accurate. Anna O. had had an attack of abdominal cramps (caused by a childbirth fantasy), and Freud later recalled her words, reported to him by Breuer, which he had not understood at first. She had said, "Now Dr. Breuer's child is coming." On June 2, 1932 (half a century later!), Freud wrote to Stefan Zweig:

> At this moment he held in his hand the key that would have opened the "doors to the Mothers" [allusion to an image in Goethe's *Faust*], but he let it drop. With all his great intellectual gifts there was nothing Faustian in his nature. Seized by conven-

tional horror he took flight and abandoned the patient to a colleague. For months afterwards she struggled to regain her health in a sanatorium.[22]

Bertha Pappenheim later distinguished herself in Germany by founding the first organizations for social work. Technically she was not completely "cured," but as often happens—and thanks partly to Breuer—she had transformed a literally paralyzing neurosis into a source of usable energy.

Ten years later, in 1892, Freud was no more capable of picking up this key that had eluded Breuer, and did not have the slightest idea of doing it. His goal at that time was to have the authenticity of hysterical and hypnotic symptoms recognized, to find a theoretical explanation for them, to perfect a therapeutic technique by taking what he could from Charcot, Bernheim . . . and Breuer! He could not wait; Janet, who had entered the Salpêtrière after Freud had left, had already published *Psychological Automatism* in 1889 and was to publish *The Mental State of Hysterics* in 1893. It was therefore imperative to prepare quickly to publish the "Preliminary Communication" on psychic mechanisms of hysterical phenomena. It cannot be denied that at the time there was a certain resemblance between Breuer's and Janet's ideas, although there can be no question of priority since Breuer was treating Anna O. at a time when Janet was yet to see a hysterical patient. Janet's secondary states corresponded slightly to hypnoid states, but because Janet had taken the position of permanently burying, so to speak, the problems of hysteria within the mystery of an "insufficiency," which suggests recourse to organicity, one cannot see how his theory could have developed, whereas the position of Breuer and Freud was open to necessary progress from the beginning. As often happens with those who are on the verge of a discovery, Freud was fearful that Janet would make it before he did, if he had enough time. When Freud received *Neurosis and Fixed Ideas* (1898), he remarked in a letter to Fliess: "I picked up a recent book of Janet's on hysteria and *idées fixes* with beating heart, and laid it down again with my pulse returned to normal. He has no suspicion of the clue."[23]

In 1893, resemblances between the two theories were due to the fact that the description of phenomena obtained in hypnosis still occupied a major place in publications; but the essential factors, namely that a therapeutic effect was obtained by having the dominant fantasy expressed in words, that the cure itself was the means of research and served as a control for hypotheses, remained foreign to Janet. One still finds today, among psychologists, objectors who lament that psychoanalysis makes no room for "objective observation." This is going back to Janet, seventy years late.

In the "Preliminary Communication," in addition to Breuer's hypnoid states, there appeared Freud's theory of *defense*, that is to say, *repression*. It stated that there were things the patient wanted to forget and therefore intentionally pushed back, repressing them from his consciousness. (That idea had already appeared in a paper by Freud a year before.) Freud still believed that there were not two theories but two varieties of hysteria. The major point was that the *separated* state (hypnoid or repressed) must come back to consciousness, provoking an affective discharge (abreaction), as if the solution of a problem had been found or a foreign body eliminated. We know from his correspondence that the idea of abreaction had its origin in an unverifiable theoretical postulate: the function of the psychical apparatus is to release nervous excitations in order to maintain them at the lowest level. That was the principle of "constancy." Freud always remained faithful to it, because it had played an important role in the theoretical orientations of the beginning. But it was to have fewer and fewer practical applications. It is piously preserved in temples of analysis; in actual fact, it is little used.

In describing her states as "clouds" or "stupors," Anna O. was probably the inventor of "hypnoid states." But what had to be explained (the idea of the unconscious was still quite vague) was the division of consciousness. Freud's explanation of repression was that the subject tries to get rid of an "incompatible" idea *voluntarily*.

> That idea is not annihilated by a repudiation of this kind, but merely repressed into the unconscious. . . . the actual outcome is something different from what the subject intended. What he wanted was to do away with an idea, as though it had never appeared, but all he succeeds in doing is to isolate it psychically.[24]

He compared that attitude to a lack of moral courage, to an ostrich policy. (From it would evolve the concept of *resistance*, obviously linked at first to the fact that its technique, as it was then, involved encouragement and "pressure.") As for the concept of the unconscious, it was not yet implied in the word "unconscious" as used in the above quotation. The existence of *an unconscious* could only be presumed. Freud informed us of the difficulty: when the patients, having recognized the truth of an interpretation, add, "But I can't *remember* having thought it."

It is easy to come to terms with them by telling them
that the thoughts were *unconscious*. But how is this
state of affairs to be fitted into our own psychological views? Are we to disregard this withholding
of recognition on the part of patients, when, now that
the work is finished, there is no longer any motive
for their doing so? [They have recognized the truth
of the interpretation, but not the existence of the
thought.] Or are we to suppose that we are really
dealing with thoughts which never came about,
which merely had a *possibility* of existing, so that the
treatment would lie in the accomplishment of a
psychical act which did not take place at the time?
It is clearly impossible to say anything about this
—that is, about the state which the pathogenic material was in before the analysis—until we have arrived
at a thorough clarification of our basic psychological
views, especially on the nature of consciousness.[25]

Clarification has not entirely eliminated the question; as
late as 1937, a remarkable echo could be found in a paper
on "Constructions in Analysis" (and perhaps also in the
1925 paper on "Negation").

But what is already decisive is the affirmation of
what can be called the axiom of identity in psychoanalysis: "But the physical process which underlies an
idea is the same in content and form (though not in
quantity) whether the idea rises above the threshold of
consciousness or remains beneath it."[26] That axiom would
necessitate the recognition of an unconscious, and the
knowledge of that unconscious would necessitate the
clear definition of the axiom.

In 1923, Freud did not repudiate the 1895 work:

The cathartic method was the immediate precursor

of psycho-analysis; and, in spite of every extension of experience and of every modification of theory, is still contained within it as its nucleus. But it was no more than a new medical procedure for influencing certain nervous diseases, and nothing suggested that it might become a subject for the most general interest and for the most violent contradiction.[27]

With *Studies on Hysteria*, a number of points were established. In particular, the abandonment of hypnosis and suggestion led to the discovery of the "free association" method. Two vital comments on suggestion and hypnosis: Patients who stubbornly defended their symptoms against all suggestions turned as docile as the best hospital subject when the suggestions bore on insignificant things. As for hypnosis without suggestion such as Breuer used, it had two inconveniences: it succeeded only with some subjects, and the results were not lasting (because resistances had been avoided instead of being analyzed).

Another important comment was made at the beginning of the crucial analysis in the case of Elisabeth von R.

I have not always been a psychotherapist. Like other neuropathologists, I was trained to employ local diagnoses and electro-prognosis, and it still strikes me myself as strange that the case histories I write should read like short stories and that, as one might say, they lack the serious stamp of science. I must console myself with the reflection that the nature of the subject is evidently responsible for this, rather than any preference of my own. . . . a detailed description of mental processes such as we are accustomed to find in the works of imaginative writers enables me, with the use of a few psychological formulas, to obtain at least some kind of insight into the course of that affection.[28]

Thus, the hypothesis that it was sufficient to recall to consciousness forgotten memories in order to eliminate them "like foreign bodies" took on another—still obscure, although familiar—dimension. But Freud was not to follow the route of an "existential" analysis. He held together the different levels and moved the existential and what he would later call the "metapsychological" aspects ahead side by side.

Breuer's way of theorizing was much simpler, for he was only looking for general laws to explain the clinical material. Freud was not satisfied with that; he had to have models. And later, metapsychology did not excuse him from also making a place for oaths, treason, fate, myths, etc. Metapsychology was to take the place that German writers had given to neurology, but it was to become the theoretical basis, the foundation upon which many other things would evolve.

Two major questions were posed in passing in *Studies on Hysteria*, without revealing the importance that they were to acquire: transference and sexuality.

Sexuality

The idea of infantile sexuality was not accessible as long as the trauma theory remained dominant. According to that theory, neurotics were traumatized in childhood by actual attempts at sexual seduction, at an age when their sexuality was not yet awakened; in puberty, the awakening

of sexuality rendered the *memory* of the trauma pathogenic. Only the discovery of the Oedipus complex eliminated this theoretical construction. But in the *Studies*
it was already recognized clinically that the "incompatible" memories that formed the core of repression were
the sexual memories.

Faced with that question, Breuer was embarrassed
and ambiguous. He had written earlier that there was no
trace of sexuality in Anna O., and he certainly ought to
have been aware of the facts.

On November 8, 1895 (the *Studies* had appeared in
May), Freud wrote to Fliess:

> Not long ago Breuer made a big speech to the phy-
> sicians' society about me, putting himself forward as
> a convert to belief in sexual aetiology. When I
> thanked him privately for this he spoiled my pleasure
> by saying: "But all the same I *don't* believe it!" Can
> you make head or tail of that? I cannot.[29]

However, Freud in the *Studies* had just spoken of
"the strange state of mind in which one knows and does
not know a thing at the same time . . . that blindness of
the seeing eye which is so astonishing in the attitude of
mothers to their daughters, husbands to their wives and
rulers to their favorites."[30] He was to take up the complex
question of not-knowing again in 1927 and in 1938, in
two papers on fetishism and the splitting of the ego.

What had happened to Breuer had already happened
before, but Freud was not to understand this until much
later.

In 1905, at a time when his theory of sexuality was
earning him general hostility, Freud said that certain

memories were coming back to him. Three men (Breuer, Charcot, and Chrobak) had imparted to him a knowledge that strictly speaking they did not possess. Breuer had explained the condition of a certain patient as due to "boudoir secrets." Charcot, in speaking of a similar case, had exclaimed, "But in such cases, it is always the genital thing, always, always!" Chrobak (an eminent gynecologist), more outspoken, had stated that it was impossible to give a hysteric the only effective prescription: "*Penis normalis*. Renewable . . ." Subsequently questioned (except for Charcot, who was dead), they denied ever having made such statements. All of which, Freud tells us, astonished him greatly. He did not think that, like the others, he knew without knowing! He acted as if he himself did not suspect anything. He curiously chose to play—and in a way embarrassing to his biographers— the role of the innocent confronted by "the clever ones" who know how to play non-knowledge against knowledge. Invoking Freud's scientific integrity is not sufficient: with the others, science was separate from a worldly knowing. But "naïveté," in the proper sense of the word, prevented Freud from practicing that form of duplicity, that "splitting." It opposed him to the "honest" Breuer, whose honesty was founded on that duplicity. In any case, it is simplistic, and more angelic than analytic, to suppose that Freud had a pure soul because of undemanding sexual "instincts."

Perhaps Breuer's ambiguous attitude, which resembled a lack of character, had something to do with the fact that Freud eventually quarreled with him. Freud's dislike for Breuer was to be very strong for a while, and there may have been other reasons for it. Not only did Freud owe him much, besides money, but Freud also often reversed his attachments this way, repeating, he said, his conduct at age three toward his nephew. The men from whom he became estranged (Fliess, Jung) were those from whom he had expected much at first. An "irrational" element, which the elucidation of transference was to clarify much later, was at work there, and with special violence.

"My Other Self . . ."

Freud's long friendship with Fliess did not chronologically follow his friendship with Breuer. It began in 1887, through a real *coup de foudre*. Much later Freud would remind Fliess that at the beginning of their relationship he was nothing but an "oto-rhino" (throat-ear physician). But in 1887 Freud greatly admired him.

Psychoanalysis would not be what it is today without that encounter. The influence of Charcot and Breuer on Freud belongs to the history of ideas. Fliess's contribution would figure strangely in such a history. How, for example, could what he called "the role of nasal mucous lining in hysteria" figure in it? And yet, Fliess's influence was greater than Breuer's! With Breuer Freud learned many things; but with Fliess, he made his own analysis and in a way established a model for analysis that subsequent analyses could repeat.

Fliess, although two years younger than Freud, had made greater progress in his life and in his profession. It is certain that Freud saw in him an idealized image of himself. Indeed, he called him "my other self." We have a photograph of the two friends side by side. Despite different facial features, the resemblance is nonetheless so striking as to evoke a smile. And then, no analyst could overlook the impression produced by the name: behind the name of Fliess there is Fleischl, and even further back perhaps Fluss . . . we know that later Freud would make use of these similarities, explaining Napoleon's love for Josephine by his attachment to his brother Joseph. The analysis of his patients (or his own?) had shown him the importance of such coincidences.

We know quite well the course of Freud's friendship for Fliess, although all the letters have not been published. Here we enter into the paradoxes and subtleties of an analytic situation which, of course, was not recognized as such. For some unknown reason, Freud treated Fliess as "a man assumed to be knowledgeable" (as Jacques Lacan says) and expected him to know about things with which he did not have the slightest acquaintance. The result was that Fliess would create for himself a knowledge which—without too much twisting of the meaning of words, but not more, in any case, than Freud was to do with the "Rat Man"—might be called "delirious." One can easily discern here the classic themes which could be the result of a poorly resolved castration complex. There are three themes tied together: (1) All humans or all living things are subject to a precise law of periodicity, on the model of menstrual periods. (2) All humans are physiologically bisexual. (3) The nose has the same structure as the genitals. In 1892, Fliess published a book on the therapy of the nasal-reflex neurosis where he set forth these ideas. In the transferential position in which he was, Freud admired and adopted them. Paradoxically that attitude proved to be much more fruitful than if he had criticized and rejected them! For those ideas were made —unwittingly—out of the same cloth as analysis. Freud accepted them as scientific truths, as the word of a physician, and not as the delirium of a sick man. But that scarcely matters. What counts is that with these ideas we enter into a very special domain, one he had not discovered with Breuer, where knowledge is produced by the accidents of unconscious desire. Thanks to Freud, Fliess's ideas acquired a future: the theory of bisexuality was to be the basis of the first explanation of homosexuality and suggest the concept of component drives, indispensable to the structure of *Three Essays on the Theory of Sexuality* (1905). The sexual symbolism of the nose was to become the model of a type of displacement encountered every day in analysis. Periodicity embarrassed Freud for a long time, but it was to find its place in the form of the very important concept of repetition.

There is no doubt that Fliess's ideas were at the root of several psychoanalytic concepts. Given the nature of psychoanalysis, it is not surprising that Freud was able to extract truths from such aberrant notions. And perhaps he remembered, while writing in London at the end of his life, the strange experience he had undergone: "For a patient never forgets again what he has experienced in the form of transference; it carries a greater force of conviction than anything he can acquire in other ways."[31]

Periodicity was tied to the idea of death (as repetition would later be). In the name of that theory, Fliess must have made some imprudent prediction which, in the transferential situation, assumed the force of a prophecy. Be that as it may, Freud believed that the date of his death was fixed for 1907. In 1901, in regard to his interest in calculations made by the unconscious, he would write:

I generally come upon speculations about the duration of my own life and the lives of those dear to me; and the fact that my friend in B[erlin] has made the periods of human life the subject of his calculations, which are based on biological units, must have acted as a determinant of this unconscious juggling. I am not now in agreement with one of the premisses from which this work of his proceeds; from highly egoistic motives [to live longer!] I should be very glad to carry my point against him, and yet I appear to be imitating his calculations in my own way.[32]

It would be truthful to say that Freud radically and in the most valuable way transformed Fliess's ideas, but that he never completely lost his interest in them. Indeed, there was a time when he took them to be his own and actually presented them to Fliess as such, to the great astonishment of the latter. A severe case of amnesia, according to Jones. More likely, the logical outcome of a nearly total identification. It was during this extraordinarily troubled period—that is to say, troubled in the manner of a "going" analysis—that Freud made the most important discoveries and had the kind of intuitions he characterized as occurring only once in a lifetime. Breuer's knowledge in matters of psychotherapy may have been an indispensable contribution and a useful preparation for Freud, but Fliess's ignorance led him to take the decisive steps.

Death—still unacknowledged by Freud, who was to wonder much later about the nature of the resistance that had hidden it from him for so long—now came to the forefront. Manifestations which would be (quite wrongly) called psychosomatic today made him Fliess's patient. He suspected Fliess of hiding from him the fatal illness from which he suffered and had resigned himself to death. It was not possible, at the time, to suspect in his attitude the effects of transference. His "cure" (of a pseudocardiac condition) came about by the process of self-recognition as a hysteric (a delayed effect of identification with Charcot's patients), namely by presenting himself as a "patient" in another way.

But first, in order to escape what would finally be the path to salvation, in a last effort of *resistance* he threw himself into a vast theoretical work, which he pursued feverishly and suddenly abandoned. This was the *"Psychology for Neurologists"*—eventually to be published as an Appendix to the Fliess letters. In it can be seen an attempt to pursue Charcot's research on an entirely new basis. Charcot had no original psychology; in this area he accepted the knowledge of his time. His neurology was stamped by prevailing psychological preconceptions; the final aim was to rediscover in cerebral anatomy the blueprint for a veritable psychological *ideology*. His discoveries owed their importance to the actual observations he was able to make in pursuit of that visionary goal. But for Charcot there were, properly speaking, no psychological problems. Normal psychology presented no difficulties. When it was abnormal, the cause had to be found in a neuropathologic factor. Freud had more subtle ideas on psychology as well as on neurology.

The "Project"—as it is generally referred to—he sent to Fliess is difficult reading, even now when we have at our disposal to understand it major help from all later writings. Essentially, the aim was to present the psychological theory in a form that could be read in neurological language, the hypothetical language of a neurology yet to be constructed. The soundest ideas of the "Project" were taken up again in Chapter 7 of *The Interpretation of Dreams*, and there one can see more clearly what Freud needed: a model functioning like a machine but in effect a fictitious one, without any relation to anything neurological. (Thus it can be said that metapsychology took the place occupied by neurology.)

But in 1895, soon after the publication of the *Studies*, the enterprise was premature and the real obstacles were elsewhere. The indisputable theoretical value of some of its elaborations does not hide the fact that the "Project" played a role of resistance in the very midst of the Fliess relationship. Indeed, the proof is that such a resistance was openly revealed as soon as the "Project," which concealed it, was abandoned: Freud found himself in a state he described as "extraordinary." Theoretical work was no longer possible. Ideas emerged and disappeared; everything was in doubt. On June 12, 1897, he wrote Fliess: "I feel I am in a cocoon. Who knows what beast will come out of it?" Freud's letters reveal the transferential situation in which he was, but he was not able to recognize it, for it in no way corresponded to what he had heretofore called transference. We read such things as: "I had all sorts of other good ideas for you during the last few days, but they have all disappeared again. I must wait for the next drive forward, which will bring them back." Or: "I have been through some kind of a neurotic experience, with odd states of mind not intelligible to consciousness—cloudy thoughts and veiled doubts, with barely here and there a ray of light."[33]

He abandoned intellectual work which was meaningless to him; he could not force himself to do it. Ideas only came to him while daydreaming. His work with patients was closely combined with the work he was doing on himself.

> . . . I can very clearly distinguish two different intellectual states in myself. In the first I pay very careful attention to everything that my patients tell me and have new ideas during the work itself, but outside it cannot think and can do no other work. In the other I draw conclusions, make notes, have interest to spare for other things but am really farther away from things and do not concentrate properly on the work with my patients.[34]

This text, which we would like to be more detailed, is worth considering by anyone who wonders about the origin of fleeting attention.

Freud's own analysis was being made along with that of his patients.

> Also the fellow is feeling shamelessly well. He has demonstrated the truth of my theories in my own person, for with a surprising turn he provided me with the solution of my own railway phobia (which I had overlooked). . . . My phobia, if you please, was a poverty, or rather a hunger phobia, arising out of my infantile gluttony and called up by the circumstances that my wife had no dowry (of which I am proud).[35]

What has been called Freud's self-analysis—as he himself called it for several weeks (*Selbstanalyse*)—was simply the discovery of analysis. On July 7, 1897, he described the transference in very clear terms, without theoretically recognizing it.

I still do not know what has been happening to me. Something from the deepest depths of my own neurosis has ranged itself against my taking a further step in understanding of the neuroses, and you have somehow been involved. My inability to write seems to be aimed at hindering our intercourse. I have no proofs of this, but merely feelings of a very obscure nature.

[He added, like a patient in analysis:]
No doubt the heat and overwork have contributed.[36]

Oedipus

A short but decisive and profound crisis took place beginning in 1896. The Oedipus complex had already appeared incognito, under the form of "real" transgression, that of incest, and still more disguised under the aspect of the trauma created by the seduction of a child by an adult. That trauma was the essential part of the etiology of hysteria: the repressed memory of the trauma became pathogenic at puberty. (Thus, neurosis had its origin in childhood—its sexual character was justified, but the unpleasant notion of infantile sexuality was avoided.) Freud had drawn this hypothesis from a small number of actual cases, and from many cases where there were only fantasies. In reality, the etiological hypothesis was but the resistance that protected him from the knowledge of unconscious oedipal desires.

But Freud noticed the fantasy character of the seductions that hysterical adults related having been subjected to in their childhood. Everything seemed to crumble; his theory of hysteria did not hold. He tried to salvage something from it: "Fantasies related to things the child had heard early in life, and whose meaning he could only understand later . . ." Thus the child's innocence was once more preserved; the memory became pathogenic at puberty.

The new theory of fantasy was roughly correct; it is the one found in the case of the "Wolf Man," and furthermore, it subtends the whole discussion of the primal scene. But in 1897, Freud could no longer believe in his "neurotica," if the reality of the trauma were taken away from him. He then felt himself in a "strange" state of both confusion and triumph. He no longer knew where he was, nor what he was going to do, but he wrote:

> Were I depressed, jaded, unclear in my mind, such doubts might be taken for signs of weakness. But as I am in just the opposite state, I must acknowledge them to be the result of honest and effective intellectual labor, and I am proud that after penetrating so far I am still capable of such criticism. Can these doubts be only an episode on the way to further knowledge? [He knew the answer was yes.]
>
> It is curious that I feel not in the least disgraced, though the occasion might seem to require it. Certainly I shall not tell it in Gath, or publish it in the streets of Askalon, in the land of the Philistines—but between ourselves I have a feeling more of triumph than of defeat (which cannot be right).[37]

The last parenthesis expresses a sort of superstitious drawing back before a feeling of triumph.

Basically, the problem facing Freud had an unfortunate precedent: the discovery that electrotherapy had no scientific foundation. However, one had to earn a living! "It is a pity one cannot live on dream interpretation . . ." (Freud was beginning to understand his own dreams in 1895.)

He would not completely give up the idea of the trauma, and later he would try again to anchor fantasy in a reality of early childhood, or even of prehistory. But first the trauma theory had to be surmounted, for it stood in the way of the Oedipus complex.

The perception of the oedipal drama, four months before the abandonment of the trauma, occurred in a dream—as in Sophocles; and as in Sophocles, that dream was interpreted in such a way as to mask the truth.

> Not long ago I dreamt that I was feeling over-affectionately towards Mathilde, but her name was "Hella," and then I saw the word "Hella" in heavy type before me. The solution is that Hella is the name of an American niece whose photograph we have been sent. Mathilde may have been called Hella because she has been weeping so bitterly recently over the Greek defeats. . . . The dream of course fulfills my wish to pin down a father as the originator of neurosis and put an end to my persistent doubts.[38]

That analysis showed, in an exceptionally clear way, how it was indeed the theory of trauma, of the seduction by the father, which served as defense against knowledge of the Oedipus complex. The "persistent doubts" (after awakening) were the fear that that dream might reveal a desire for Mathilde. If it revealed another desire, that the trauma be verified, then it was much more reassuring. For us, who know what was to follow, it is clear that such a defense could not have lasted very long. It is quite easy for us afterwards to play the role of Tiresias. But Freud played that of Oedipus! Like Oedipus, he was already a great decipherer of enigmas; but he had not reached the essential and could only reach it at his own expense.

The Oedipus complex unfolded on October 15, 1897. It was, within a few days, the first anniversary of his father's death (Jakob Freud died on October 23, 1896).

Being entirely honest with oneself is a good exercise. Only one idea of general value has occurred to me. I have found love of the mother and jealousy of the father in my own case too, and now believe it to be a general phenomenon of early childhood, even if it does not always occur so early as in children who have been made hysterics. . . . If that is the case, the gripping power of *Oedipus Rex*, in spite of all the rational objections to the inexorable fate that the story presupposes, becomes intelligible, and one can understand why later fate dramas were such failures. Our feelings rise against any arbitrary, individual fate . . . but the Greek myth seizes on a compulsion which everyone recognizes because he has felt traces of it in himself. Every member of the audience was once a budding Oedipus in phantasy, and this dream-fulfillment played out in reality causes everyone to recoil in horror, with the full measure of repression which separates his infantile from his present state.

The idea has passed through my head that the same thing may lie at the root of *Hamlet*. I am not thinking of Shakespeare's conscious intentions, but supposing rather that he was impelled to write it by a real event because his own unconscious understood that of the hero. How can one explain the hysteric Hamlet's phrase "So conscience doth make cowards of us all," and his hesitation to avenge his father by kill-

ing his uncle, when he himself so casually sends his
courtiers to their death and despatches Laertes so
quickly? How better than by the torment roused in
him by the obscure memory that he himself had
meditated the same deed against his father because of
passion for his mother—"use every man after his
desert, and who should 'scape whipping?" His conscience is his unconscious feeling of guilt.[39]

Obstacles were overcome, everything was utilized,
without Freud's clearly wanting it: the fluctuations of
his transference on Fliess, the work with patients, the
fantasy relationships with the children, the death of the
father, the analysis of dreams. And, at last, an analysis
had taken place, the first one, which would be the model
for all others. Not immediately. What came from such
different sources as Breuer's experiment with Anna O.
and Freud's relationship with Fliess was not to be organized without some difficulty. That was to be done in 1907
with the "Rat Man," when everything would depend
once again on the transference of the unconscious death
wish, of which Freud was the object.

It has been said that Freud accomplished his "self-
analysis." He wrote: "I can only analyse myself with
objectively acquired knowledge (as if I were a stranger);
self-analysis is really impossible, otherwise there would
be no illness."[40] Thus, it is possible to analyze oneself—
as another—and it is not self-analysis. Fliess, without
having done anything to achieve it, by his mere existence
(he was not even there, but in Berlin) and by mobilizing
unconscious desire had made this strange adventure possible—and it is Freud who made it possible for it to be
repeated, and it is being repeated every day now, even,
naturally, among psychoanalysts who are unaware of it.

CHAPTER THREE

The Royal Road

The ANALYSIS OF DREAMS played an important role in this first analysis. But from the outset Freud saw in it another considerable advantage: the dream was a sort of normal "pathological" phenomenon, exactly the sort of normal phenomenon best calculated to help in the understanding of pathological factors. Freud was not the first to have that idea, but before him no one had known how to use it. To say that dream analysis was going to become the royal road to the unconscious had several meanings; either it was the best way to arrive at the knowledge of a patient's unconscious thoughts, or the best way to reach a theoretical knowledge of the unconscious, or the best way to bring the reading public to admit the existence of the unconscious. Naturally, these three meanings are only one. But one thing was certain: psychoanalysis was no longer confined to pathology. (Whatever that means now is far from clear! But it was in Freud's time: he believed that he would no longer be accused of elaborat-

ing theories devoid of interest for healthy people.) Thus
further inroads were made on psychiatric segregation.
Freud's path was not exactly heading in that direction,
but it had that effect. The mechanism which is at the
basis of human sacrifices—ascribing to others what one is
repressing—was revealed and the barrier, the "censorship"
or "defense," was to be installed inside everyone.

To go that far it had been necessary for Freud first
to take the patient's place—not with words, but in his
being—and to undertake to "cure" himself. In *The Interpretation of Dreams* there is an example that he in-
terprets as a "convenience" dream. It concerns a medical
student who goes back to sleep one morning instead of
going to the hospital. He then dreams that he is in a
hospital—a beautiful compromise between the wish to
sleep and the obligation to be at work, for he sees himself in bed with a card with his name written on it at
the head of the bed! But the meaning of a dream is never
exhausted in a single explanation. This one also revealed
the inevitable identification of the physician with the
patient, one that psychiatric training, and also, in a less
direct way, medical training, is aimed at overcoming.
Freud had assumed that, but now he was going to be
able to generalize and formulate a new defense, the one
A. A. Brill would use in Zurich: "Pathology" is within
the unconscious of everyone.

From the moment that Freud let his patients engage
in free association, they were bound to talk about their
dreams. He had been interested in his own, long before
he was able to understand them. On July 24, 1895, while
on vacation in Bellevue near Vienna, he succeeded in
making the first systematic or detailed, if not compre-
hensive, analysis of a dream of his which was especially

complicated and obscure. That was the dream of "Irma's injection," the first example given in *The Interpretation of Dreams*.

The idea of a complete interpretation is not very feasible. The work could go on indefinitely, or it might have to be terminated by the impossibility of continuing, and not because explanations had been exhausted. Any dream has an umbilical cord through which it communicates with the unknown. On the other hand, the interpretation clearly involves the dreamer and his most intimate thoughts, and Freud could go no further than discretion permitted where his own dreams were concerned. Thus the analysis of the dream of Irma's injection stops just at the moment when Freud had said enough to intimate that his wife was involved.

For these reasons, and also because he wanted to study dreams for their own sake, without tying them to the analysis of the dreamer (although he often failed to follow it, Freud had made it a rule for himself to refer only to dreams of "normal" subjects), *The Interpretation of Dreams* somewhat resembles selections of texts used in language study. One knows only as much of each story as is necessary for its interpretation.

On January 3, 1899, when the book was finished except for the very important seventh and last chapter, he wrote Fliess:

> . . . the dream pattern is capable of universal application, and . . . the key to hysteria really lies in dreams. I understand now why, in spite of all my efforts, I was unable to finish the dream book. If I wait a little longer I shall be able to describe the mental process in dreams in such a way as to include the process in hysterical symptom-formation. So let us wait.[41]

What was still needed to finish the book was the theory of the functioning of the psychical "apparatus." At the same time, the work was interminable: new ideas that made him go beyond his initial project came to Freud endlessly, and he agreed to enlarge it so as to offer a more general theory than he had originally foreseen. In the preface to the first edition he would also say:

> . . . the dream is the first member of a class of abnormal psychical phenomena of which further members, such as hysterical phobias, obsessions and delusions, are bound for practical reasons to be a matter of concern to physicians. As will be seen in the sequel, dreams can make no such claim to practical importance; but their theoretical value as a paradigm is on the other hand proportionately greater. Anyone who has failed to explain the origin of dream-images can scarcely hope to understand phobias, obsessions or delusions or to bring a therapeutic influence to bear on them.[42]

To say that the dream is a paradigm is to say that the explanation of the dream will serve as a model for the explanation of symptoms. But another as yet barely glimpsed idea may also be present. The dream itself is a model of hallucination, of delirium, as mourning was to become the model of melancholia. Besides, later (in 1917) Freud was to bring together these states—dream, sleep, love, mourning—which have in common, above all, that they are normal and also exceptions to habitual psychic states, but they were to be grouped together for yet another reason, after the concept of narcissism had been formulated.

The Interpretation of Dreams, like several of Freud's other books, consisted of a large collection of examples followed by a theoretical chapter. Indeed, that composition gives an idea of Freud's method of work, inherited partly from Charcot but perhaps also from his laboratory work: to look at things long enough so that they begin to "speak." Examples were divided into several classes, each serving to illustrate one hypothesis: The dream represents the fulfillment of a desire, and its elaboration is made by means of condensation, displacement, etc. In the theoretical conclusions of the final chapter, Freud again returned to the 1895 "Project," not abandoning his concern about explaining quantitatively the circulation of psychical charges. But that kind of explanation was now pushed from the foreground into the background. A mechanism with unconscious desire as its driving force was now surreptitiously taking over the place formerly occupied by those constructions Freud had described with neurological concepts at the back of his mind.

The text of the dream, as the dreamer presents it, has often been compared, first by Freud himself, to a text to be translated.

The dream-thoughts and the dream-content are presented to us like two versions of the same subject-matter in two different languages. Or, more properly, the dream-content seems like a transcript of the dream-thoughts into another mode of expression, whose characters and syntactic laws it is our business to discover by comparing the original and the translation.[43]

Let us immediately make the obvious but often neglected remark: The "thought" of the dream is in itself clear and "logical"; it is not the unconscious, although it is unconscious; it is the text of the dream which is

marked by the work of the unconscious. By analyzing
the dream we clearly obtain the unconscious thought
that was hidden from us, in the way that we rediscover
a forgotten memory. But it is the text, with its distortions,
that will inform us about the "syntax" of the unconscious.
In that stated position the whole theory of the 1905 book
on jokes was already in embryo. One cannot read *The
Interpretation of Dreams* as a key to dreams and say to
oneself after each interpreted dream: "So! That's what
it means," and believe that what it meant is what Freud
had in mind when he spoke of the unconscious. True,
he had not yet made the differentiation between the
different meanings of the word "unconscious," and thus
was exposing himself to misinterpretation.

At first sight, therefore, the manifest text of the
dream refers to a latent thought, almost as a modified,
censored, falsified text would refer to the original text
that is to be reconstituted. This is certainly not the work
involved in translation! At least, those who do that sort
of work on ancient documents do not call themselves
translators. One would have a more accurate idea, although it is only an analogy, if one demonstrated how
one could reconstitute the original Latin by starting with
a poor translation by a student: for example, rediscover
summa diligentia, having at one's disposal only "the top
of the stagecoach," but using all the means, the context,
the phonetic similarities, and so forth. If that work was
carried out comprehensively it would teach us according
to what rules poor students translate Latin, in the way
that dream analysis informs us on the work of the unconscious. This is only a comparison. But to say that
dreams are texts to be translated is also a rough approxi-
mation.

Of course, the story told by the dreamer has no

meaning in itself, and the rules according to which it has been transformed are not those that regulate our discourse in the waking state. But the mechanisms of the dream, according to Freud, are much more complicated than the reconstitution of a text. Symbolism, censorship, thoughts expressed in the form of images, are only avenues of approach. An unconscious desire, going back to childhood and awakened by an actual present desire, is "transferred" into a "normal" thought, carries the latter away, and "plunges" it into the world of the unconscious, where it is subjected to the laws of syntax in force there (the laws of the *primary process*). At the same time, that dream thought follows a path which leads it to the end of the psychical apparatus (fictitious, not neurological) in charge of perception. Thereby the thought becomes perception, that is to say, *hallucination* of a scene which more or less overtly represents the fulfillment of the desire.

The limits of this modest study rule out my attracting the reader, as into a trap, into the fearsome complications of Freudian metapsychology, which is not a reason to completely hide them from him as has often been done in popularizing works. We will come to their easier aspects when we examine examples of dreams. However, the role played by language in that process cannot be neglected: the dream thought has a verbal form. Freud was obliged to postulate the concept of the *preconscious*, which is in charge of words. The primary process translates words into images, like a maker of rebuses, and thus the dream must not be interpreted as a painting would be but as the visual representation of the words themselves.

The Interpretation of Dreams was written during a crisis that resulted from the turbulence of the Fliess relationship and the ordeal of Freud's father's death. Solutions emerged during the course of the work. That is why it is the easiest book of all his works for making Freud contradict himself. But it is also the book wherein the unconscious was revealed, and no other work of Freud's would ever again have the same impact.

In summing up what has been said before, let us in any case remember this key statement, that "a normal train of thought is only submitted to abnormal psychical treatment of the sort we have been describing, that of dreams and hysteria [and it would have to be added later, of obsessional neurosis] if an unconscious wish, derived from infancy and in a state of repression, has been transferred on to it."[44]

The widespread misconception that the dream thought and its interpretation come from the "depths" of the unconscious is traceable to the survival of a remnant of Platonism (thoughts come from the soul and seek a language to express themselves) and also to a mystical orientation (there must be in the deepest center of ourselves a mystery which is a kind of revelation). It is precisely on this point that Jung was to secede from Freud; he made analysis into a hermeneutics in order to read the great revelations of the unconscious, whereas all that Freud sought therein was a normal thought repressed and transformed by the work of the primary process.

The primary process and its laws are recognized above all in the use the dream makes of condensation and displacement. Condensation fuses several ideas of the thought into a single image of the manifest content (for example, one person in the dream could be interpreted as representing two or more persons) and displacement represents one word by another. For example, it could be shown that a person appearing casually in the dream might be, let us say, the mother of the dreamer, because her image has something in common with that of the mother. These mechanisms of the unconscious are also very clearly seen in lapses and puns, as well as in ordinary speech, in the form of figures of speech (metaphors and metonymy, for example). The influence of the unconscious, dominant in the dream, is present at every moment. The study of dreams therefore has considerable portent. It poses decisive questions for language in general, and they are questions that a unilinear concept of speech does not allow to be posed. The unconscious too easily appears to be a thing we speak about, while actually it speaks in its specific way and with its specific syntax. As Jacques Lacan has said, it is "structured like a language."

As we have seen, the fact that the dream expresses itself in images does not mean that condensation and displacement cannot affect verbal elements. It is because Professor Gärtner (meaning "gardener") had a *blooming* wife (which might encourage one to try to make a pun) that the dream presented a picture from a botanical monograph (in the dream called "The Botanical Monograph"). Such examples are legion. Even in the earlier *Studies on Hysteria*, we find that Elisabeth von R. dreamed she saw two physicians (Breuer and Freud) *hanging* side by side —which meant that one was not worth any more than the other—just as, in their association, they *hung* around together. Another patient—and in this instance it is no longer a dream but a symptom, although the formation law is the same—was unable to walk, apparently for physical reasons. And it becomes apparent that it was because she did not feel herself on an "equal footing" with others. Breuer, through excessive fidelity to his hypnoid states, was close to Janet's concept of psychasthenia when he explained those traits by a simple failure of the critical sense tied to those states. Fliess reproached Freud for basing his explanations on puns, and later his patients, for example the "Rat Man," would tell him in the face of such interpretations: "It is too superficial. I cannot believe it." But Freud was adamant. He maintained that every time a psychical element is tied to another element by a questionable and superficial association, there will also exist between them a legitimate and deeper bond which is subject to resistance and censorship. Analysis shows that there can be considerable distance between the "questionable" and the legitimate thought. Thus, the "superficial" association *Gärtner-botanical-blooming* is explained, but only in the end, by the "legitimate" thought: "I sacrifice too much to my fantasy," which seems at first sight singularly far-fetched.

The problem Freud posed, which is not yet resolved, contains obscurities which are not his fault but rather that of the linguistics of his time. Freud was quick to trust the conclusions of specialists. He accepted the linguistic concepts current in that period but later abandoned, as he accepted totemism, which was fashionable with the anthropologists of that time. Today, when linguists and anthropologists criticize Freud for his attitude toward linguistics or anthropology, they do not see beyond the internal problems of their specialty. It was not Freud's aim to sustain these concepts that have been abandoned. When the linguists affirmed that words were sensorial images of a certain type (naturally, this was also Charcot's viewpoint), images of "things" which functioned as meaningful, Freud could believe them but he was not deceived by them. He only needed a dualism—besides manifest language he had to have another; and he never thought, as did the linguists of his time, that images are what words speak about, for, in their way, they are words themselves. The questions he implicitly posed for the linguists of his time remain posed for those of today.

Uncle Josef

An example of dream analysis must be given. I shall choose one which is simple and short in its manifest statement, so that the examination of that statement will detain us as little as possible.

In 1897, when the dream took place, Freud had just been recommended for appointment as Professor Extraordinary at the University of Vienna. He had few illusions; one of his colleagues, R., had not been able to get nominated because, like Freud, he was a Jew.

The day after Freud had spoken about the question of nominations with R., he had the following dream:

I. . . . My friend R. was my uncle.—I had a great feeling of affection for him.
II. I saw before me his face, somewhat changed. It was as though it had been drawn out lengthways. A yellow beard that surrounded it stood out especially clearly.[45]

(The first part is a thought, the second an image. Dreams, as we know from our own experience, are not made up solely of images.)

The manifest content did not excite his curiosity in any particular way. He had forgotten it when he woke up, and he burst out laughing when it came back to mind. He thought it was absurd and not worth an analysis.

But it refused to go away and followed me about all day, till at last in the evening I began to reproach myself: "If one of your patients who was interpreting a dream could find nothing better to say than that it was nonsense, you would take him up about it and suspect that the dream had some disagreeable story at the back of it which he wanted to avoid becoming aware of. Treat yourself in the same way. Your opinion that the dream is nonsense only means that you have an internal resistance against interpreting it."[46]

He therefore started the analysis. In order to do that, he considered the dream piece by piece. He began with the uncle. He had several uncles, but the one who came to mind was his uncle Josef. What "association" could there be with Uncle Josef? Well, thirty years before, Uncle Josef had been dishonest and had been punished by the law. His brother (Freud's father) had been greatly worried by this affair and he used to excuse Josef by saying that he was not bad, but only a simpleton.

So that if my friend R. was my Uncle Josef, what I was meaning to say was that R. was a simpleton. Hardly credible and most disagreeable![47]

The face in the dream and the color of the beard were like a combination of R. and Uncle Josef—a *condensation*. The importance of the beard—its particular color—must be a *displacement*. (Freud remarks on this but does not explain it. That must have been too personal.)

I still had no idea at all what could be the purpose of this comparison, against which I continued to struggle. It did not go very deep, after all, since my uncle was a criminal, whereas my friend R. bore an unblemished character . . . except for having been fined for knocking a boy down with his bicycle. Could I have had that crime in mind? That would have been making fun of the comparison. At this point I remembered another conversation which I had had a few days earlier with another colleague, N., and, now I came to think of it, upon the same subject. I had met N. in the street. He too had been recommended for a professorship. He had heard of the honour that had been paid me and had offered me his congratulations on it; but I had unhesitatingly refused to accept them. "You are the last person," I had said, "to make that kind of joke; you know what such a recommendation is worth from your own experience." "Who can say?" he had answered— jokingly, it seemed; "there was something definite against *me*. Don't you know that a woman once started legal proceedings against me? I needn't assure you that the case was dismissed. It was a disgraceful attempt at blackmail; and I had the greatest difficulty in saving the prosecutrix from being punished. But perhaps they may be using this at the Ministry as an excuse for not appointing me. But *you* have an un-blemished character." This told me who the criminal was, and at the same time showed me how the dream was to be interpreted and what its purpose was. My Uncle Josef represented my two colleagues who had not been appointed to professorships—the one as a simpleton and the other as a criminal. I now saw too why they were represented in this light. If the ap-pointment of my friends R. and N. had been post-poned for "denominational" reasons, my own ap-pointment was also open to doubt; if, however, I could attribute the rejection of my two friends to other reasons, which did not apply to me, my hopes would remain untouched.[48]

All the material has not yet been interpreted, far from it. What has been discovered is Freud's desire that the failures of his colleagues be explained by reasons that were not valid for him. In the interests of that wish, how offhandedly, with what egotism he treated his colleagues! He *sacrificed* them to his desire. (It is easier to excuse him if we admit that the dream uses those faces as simple means of expression . . .)

I then recalled that there was still a piece of the dream which the interpretation had not touched. After the idea had occurred to me that R. was my uncle, I had had a warm feeling of affection for him in the dream. Where did that feeling belong? I had naturally never had any feeling of affection for my Uncle Josef. I had been fond of my friend R. and had esteemed him for many years; but if I had gone up to him and expressed my sentiments in terms approaching the degree of affection I had felt in the dream, there could be no doubt that he would have been astonished. My affection for him struck me as ungenuine and exaggerated—like the judgement of his intellectual qualities which I had expressed by fusing his personality with my uncle's, though *there* the exaggeration had been in the opposite direction. But a new light began to dawn on me. The affection in the dream did not belong to the latent content, to the thoughts that lay behind the dream; it stood in contradiction to them and was calculated to conceal the true interpretation of the dream. And probably that was precisely its *raison d'être*. I recalled my resistance against embarking on the interpreta-

tion, how long I had put it off and how I had declared that the dream was sheer nonsense. My
psycho-analytic treatments taught me how a repudiation of that kind was to be interpreted: it had no
value as a judgement but was simply an expression
of emotion. If my little daughter did not want an
apple that was offered to her, she asserted that the
apple tasted sour without having tasted it. And if
my patients behaved like the child, I knew that they
were concerned with an idea which they wanted to
repress. The same was true of my dream. I did not
want to interpret it, because the interpretation contained something that I was struggling against. When
I had completed the interpretation I learnt what it
was that I had been struggling against—namely, the
assertion that R. was a simpleton. The affection that
I felt for R. could not be derived from the latent
dream-thoughts; but no doubt it originated from this
struggle of mine. If my dream was distorted in this
respect from its latent content—and distorted into its
opposite,—then the affection that was manifest in
the dream served the purpose of this distortion.[49]

That is to say, the latent thought of the dream, namely
that R. was a simpleton—which was *desired*, because then
Freud could be nominated—was a distortion in relation
to the true feelings and true opinions of the dreamer. It
was, so to speak, an interested lie, a calumny. This calumny had to be hidden in a hypocritical way, through a
distortion in the opposite direction: the feeling of affection. But the two distortions did not come from the
same "place," from the same "agency." The calumny was
part of the thought which had been repressed. The affection was in the service of the repression. The calumny was

in the service of the desire (this was the wish to be appointed, but as we will see, an unconscious desire from childhood had been "transferred" to it), which was why it was in the latent thought. The affection only served to hide that lie, to whitewash the dreamer.

The analysis of a dream is never terminated. How could this one continue? It seemed to Freud that his desire to be appointed Professor Extraordinary was not important enough and could not have enough force to justify so many distortions. "If it was indeed true that my craving to be addressed with a different title was as strong as all that, it showed a pathological ambition which I did not recognize in myself. and which I believed was alien to me."[50]

Two memories returned to Freud's mind. He had been told that at his birth an old peasant woman predicted that he would be a great man. Later, when he was twelve years old, he remembered that a fortuneteller had predicted that he would be Prime Minister (it was the period of the *"Bürger"* Ministry). The family tradition and that personal memory helped create the hesitancy with which he had started the study of medicine; he had for some time toyed with the idea of studying law.

But now to return to my dream. It began to dawn on me that my dream had carried me back from the dreary present to the cheerful hopes of the days of the *"Bürger"* Ministry, and that the wish that it had done its best to fulfill was one dating back to those times. In mishandling my two learned and eminent colleagues because they were Jews, and in treating the one as a simpleton and the other as a criminal, I was behaving as though I were the Minister, I had put myself in the Minister's place. Turning the tables on His Excellency with a vengeance! He had refused to appoint me *professor extraordinarius* and I had retaliated in the dream by stepping into his shoes.[51]

Such an interpretation is somewhat surprising. No symbolism, no skill in divining enigmas, not even any science of unconscious thought could supply it to anyone who had the text of the dream only. There must be the associations of the dreamer himself. What it had ultimately unveiled was not so much the normal, rational thought: "I would really like to have more chances to be appointed than R. and N. have had," because that thought was neither deeply hidden nor very censorable. But that wish, attracting an older desire, subjected the thought to the dream work, to the primary process, and it came back in a form where it seemed incomprehensible. Under this new form, it revealed many unconscious thoughts; but from the unconscious it revealed only a childhood desire.

We know that Freud's ambition went back further, and even if we did not know it we could rightly think that before wishing to take the place of a minister he had wished to take the place of his father. The Oedipus complex had been discovered at the time Freud was finishing *The Interpretation of Dreams* and he gave it only a very small place in that book. But, in regard to another dream, he recalled that as a child he had urinated in his parents' bed and his father had reproached him for it. The little boy replied with a boastful offer to buy him a bed much more beautiful (red, and completely new). That original scene of ambition was not a personal memory; it had been told to him by his parents. It was later repeated:

When I was seven or eight years old . . . one evening before going to sleep I disregarded the rules which modesty lays down and obeyed the calls of nature in my parents' bedroom while they were present. In the course of his reprimand, my father let fall the words: "The boy will come to nothing." This must have been a frightful blow to my ambition, for references to this scene are still constantly recurring in my dreams and are always linked with an enumeration of my achievements and successes. . . .[52]

In passing, let us note the verification of that formula, so enigmatic at first sight: Ambition is of urethral origin.

The dream has not been completely analyzed, but it has taken us much further than we could have imagined when we started.

With the theory of dreams, the foundations of psychoanalysis were solidly established, and a great number of later works were to spring directly from it. *The Psychopathology of Everyday Life, Jokes and Their Relation to the Unconscious*, the analysis of Jensen's *Gradiva*, the case of Dora, and even more so, the case of the "Rat Man" are applications or corollaries of *The Interpretation of Dreams*.

What the discovery of the meaning of dreams has taught us is, first, the existence of the two processes, and most importantly, that the primary process is in the service of the unconscious desire. The transference of the unconscious desire into images, into "daily residues," presents a specific case, which Freud noted, where the image of the analyst functions like an ordinary "daily residue" and supports the transference of the desire. It is only a specific case Freud said, and it makes no difference whether the image of the analyst or any other image is involved. It must be understood that in effect it makes no difference from the point of view of metapsychology. It is the same mechanism. Freud had not yet theorized upon something that he had experienced with Fliess and which he would soon notice: that transference on the analyst was going to take the place of hypnosis, and that this discovery would even explain the effects of hypnosis! For Breuer hypnosis suppressed hysterical retention. For Freud, transference was evidently going to cut through resistances into the repression of unconscious desire and in that way become the instrument of the cure, as hypnosis had been for Breuer. The starting point had been the theory of the transference of the desire on the daily remnants in the dream. But there was as yet no indication of that development.

When it was published *The Interpretation of Dreams* fell into a vacuum. No one noticed that a revolution had taken place. The size of the edition was a very modest six hundred copies; it took ten years to sell them. The book provoked a few unfavorable articles, but that did not prevent its going unnoticed. It did not shock readers, it did not create a scandal as Freud's publication of 1905 would do; it was taken for a mystical book that turned its back on science. It was not understood.

The preface to the first edition was addressed to the medical world, to specialists in psychopathology. Ten years later, Freud began the preface to the second edition thus:

My psychiatric colleagues seem to have taken no trouble to overcome the initial bewilderment created by my new approach to dreams. The professional

philosophers have become accustomed to polishing
off the problems of dream-life (which they treat as
a mere appendix to conscious states) in a few sentences—and usually in the same ones; and they have
evidently failed to notice that we have something
here from which a number of inferences can be
drawn that are bound to transform our psychological
theories. The attitude adopted by reviewers in the
scientific periodicals could only lead one to suppose
that my work was doomed to be sunk into complete
silence; while the small group of gallant supporters,
who practise medical psycho-analysis under my guid-
ance and who follow my example in interpreting
dreams and make use of their interpretations in treating neurotics, would never have exhausted the first
edition of the book. Thus it is that I feel indebted
to a wider circle of educated and curious-minded
readers, whose interest has led me to take up once
more after nine years this difficult, but in many respects fundamental, work.[53]

At that time, in the summer of 1908, Freud found few
changes to be made. But he added:

For this book has a further subjective significance
for me personally—a significance which I only
grasped after I had completed it. It was, I found, a
portion of my own self-analysis, my reaction to my
father's death—that is to say, to the most important
event, the most poignant loss, of a man's life. Having
discovered that this was so, I felt unable to obliterate
the traces of the experience.[54]

It is less the fate of the book that can be followed through
the subsequent prefaces than the development of the doc-

trine. In 1911, Freud remarked that supplementary material on sexuality and symbolism was lacking in the book (he tried to add it). He foresaw what would have to be added later: a consideration of works of imagination, myths, linguistic usage, folklore. However, the text would not be further modified after this date, and after 1918, Freud decided to regard it as a "historical" document, namely, to make it the witness to the state of psychoanalysis during the time of the first three editions. Undoubtedly, the book is more than a historical witness; today it is still a basic text that cannot be ignored.

Although Freud dedicated the first edition to his colleagues and although no part of the book could have provoked protest or scandal, there was still an element of challenge in its publication. The fact that he put in the epigraph a verse from the *Aeneid*, "*Flectere si nequeo superos Acheronta movebo*,"* can be taken in different ways. It is surely an allusion to the fate of what is repressed, which, if it cannot be recognized by what Charcot called "the official consciousness," will create trouble in the depths. But Freud compared himself to the repressed; he also was prepared to raise Acheron against all resistance. If the reader doubts that the epigraph can also have that meaning, I will remind him that Freud had first chosen a quotation from Milton's *Paradise Lost* which leaves no doubt:

Let us consult

What reinforcement we may gain from hope,
If not what resolution from despair.
He preferred Virgil's verse because hell was mentioned in it.

---

* "And if Heaven be inflexible, Hell shall be unleashed!" (Trans. Jackson.)

The Psychopathology of Everyday Life

In 1901, at the request of a publisher, Freud wrote a condensed version of *The Interpretation of Dreams* in which he artfully included all the essentials in fifty pages. He returned later to the subject several times, and starting from the time when he wanted to distinguish his position from that of Jung, he insisted on the comment—which already prominently figured in *The Interpretation of Dreams*—that the function of dreams is solely to protect sleep. The function that the dream might have was not what concerned him. What he was seeking in it was a model.

In any case, in 1901 he was less concerned with continuing to study in depth his discoveries on dreams than with extending them to neighboring fields. Undoubtedly, the examples that he was going to analyze in *The Psychopathology of Everyday Life* interested him in themselves (many stories of failures or lapses resemble witticisms), which is probably why he continued to provide new examples for each new edition, which added nothing to the significance of the book. But the study proved, in an area less mysterious than dreams and one in which everyone was immediately able to verify it, the pertinency of the model constructed in relation to dreams and hysteria. Indeed, the field of "everyday pathology" was much more accessible.

As a whole, the problem faced was still roughly the same as it had been when *Studies on Hysteria* was published. At the time, Breuer spoke of the weakening of the critical sense in the "hypnoid states" and Janet of a nervous "asthenia"—in which they agreed with current thinking. Or rather, current thinking probably suspected something, but the so-called official opinion affirmed that forgetting, lapses, and so forth had no more *meaning* than faults inevitably resulting from the execution of a task; it was an echo of the old theory of the "resistance of matter" according to which an artisan, for example, could not perfectly copy a model—there would always be a small accidental difference which needed no justification. In the same way, if one word was said for another it could only be seen as an absurd accident of that kind. Freud questioned that concept and would postulate in the last chapter the thesis of absolute psychical determinism. The structure of the book was similar to that of *The Interpretation of Dreams*: a series of examples classified and interpreted, and a chapter on theory. But the theory in it was much simpler. The examples spoke for themselves and the whole was very convincing. Later, when Freud had to explain what psychoanalysis was to a lay audience, he always began with some examples borrowed from the psychopathology of everyday life because they were the most convincing.

The problem had been occupying him for some time. Two papers, one on forgetting proper names, the other on screen memories, had appeared in 1898 and 1899. Only the first was taken up again in the book; the second disguised an autobiographical episode. Freud must have been fearful that the disguise would be understood, and he utilized other less satisfactory examples. The work also studied various types of lapses, errors, failures of all kinds and, in a somewhat unexpected way, superstition in relation to number games—an echo, as we have seen, of Fliess's periodicity.

"Officially" (one does not dare say "theoretically"), lapses had no meaning, although they had long been utilized by novelists and dramatists to give a glimpse of the secret thoughts of their heroes. The hidden sense of a lapse, at least in certain simple cases, does not necessarily escape the audience. However, if that kind of hidden meaning called for a subtle response from people with an intuitive turn of mind, it had the opposite effect on the more literal-minded ones. The latter were satisfied to note resemblances between the verbal elements, and lapses were theoretically explained as errors resulting from confusion: the "thought" seized a word which was not the right one because its surface resemblance to the right one deceived it.

In the way that lapses utilize verbal elements, displacement and condensation discovered in dream analysis are easily recognized—namely, as the effects of the primary process applied to the words themselves. The question must not be simplified for, Freud said, lapses *utilize* similarities between condensed or displaced elements, they do not result from them. Besides, that similarity is not necessarily verbal; sometimes through lapses one substitutes a word for another which hardly resembles it. In Freud's own words, in words which have become inadequate, similarity can be found "in things" or "in their verbal representation." If the terminology Freud uses here belongs to an abandoned linguistic concept, the question he raises remains valid. If the traveler in Italy needs a strap and asks for *una ribera* in a shop, it is not because the correct word *corregia* resembles the word *ribera*. It is because Ribera and Corregio relate to each other as painters. In other words, somehow the lapses have an underpart, another latent unconscious *discourse*, which mingles with the manifest discourse. Taking into consideration only manifest verbal similarities, which is sufficient to explain the forgetting of proper names, is not sufficient for the study of lapses.

Naturally, if displacement and condensation are evident, it can only be as in dreams an effect, even though modified, of an unconscious desire. If Freud, on his return from vacation, dates a letter October instead of September, it is because a patient has been announced for October and Freud wants him to be there already. If an American who wants to ask his wife to join him by taking the *Mauretania* notices with some emotion that he has written *Lusitania*, his emotion is justified by the fact that his lapse reveals to him a desire that he would prefer to repress. In *The Interpretation of Dreams*, Freud points out that the "dream work," which is exercised on a "thought" which the preconscious has put in a verbal form and of which it must make a sort of riddle (the manifest content), is not set on the choice of words. It changes them as much as necessary to find similarities or irregularities in them which are favorable to its purpose. It is thus that the poet, the wit, or the jokester proceeds. We do not *make* our lapses exactly the same way. They make themselves "by themselves," but the mechanism is the same; words simply present themselves —which saves some of the work. One could speak here of a "verbal complaisance."

But if lapses show us "the other discourse" erupting in speech we thought we could control, forgetting proper names shows us the counterpart of that mechanism, for there it is the word that we thought we could control which escapes us, drawn into repression along with the unconscious discourse.

Here is the first analysis of forgetfulness of that kind:

The name that I tried without success to recall in the example I chose for analysis in 1898 was that of the artist who painted the magnificent frescoes of the "Four Last Things" in Orvieto cathedral. Instead of the name I was looking for —*Signorelli*—the names of two other painters—*Botticelli and Boltraffio*— thrust themselves on me, though they were immediately and decisively rejected by my judgement as incorrect. When I learnt the correct name from someone else, I recognized it at once and without hesitation.[55]

The "Four Last Things" are Death, Judgment, Hell, and Heaven.

At the time Freud noticed the forgetting of Signorelli's name, "which was," he said, "as familiar as one of the substitute names, and much better known than that of Boltraffio," he was traveling in a carriage from a town in Herzegovina with a casual companion. It was to that companion that he had wanted to speak about . . . the painter whose name escaped him.

Light was only thrown on the forgetting of the name when I recalled the topic we had been discussing directly before [our conversation on Italy], and it was revealed as a case in which a topic that has just been raised is disturbed by the preceding topic. . . . we had been talking about the customs of the Turks living in *Bosnia* and *Herzegovina*. I had told him what I had heard from a colleague practising among those people—that they are accustomed to show great confidence in their doctor and great resignation to fate. If one has to inform them that nothing can be done for a sick person, their reply is: "Herr [Sir], what is there to be said? If he could be saved, I know you would have saved him." In these sentences we for the first time meet with the words and names *Bosnia*, *Herzegovina* and *Herr*, which can be inserted

73

into an associative series between *Signorelli* and *Botticelli-Boltraffio*.[56]

Herr is indeed found in *Her*zegovina, but also in its translation (therefore in another way) in *Signor*elli. One must proceed a little as in the analysis of a dream by searching for associations in the manifest material. (Freud's text supposed that his companion had reminded him of the forgotten name; it is no longer the name he is looking for, but the reasons for his forgetting.)

Freud remembered that he had wanted to tell another anecdote coming from this same colleague

which lay close to the first in my memory. These Turks place a higher value on sexual enjoyment than on anything else, and in the event of sexual disorders they are plunged in a despair which contrasts strangely with their resignation towards the threat of death. One of my colleague's patients once said to him: "*Herr*, you must know that if *that* comes to an end then life is of no value." I suppressed my account of this characteristic trait, since I did not want to allude to the topic in a conversation with a stranger. But I did more: I also diverted my attention from pursuing thoughts which might have arisen in my mind from the topic of "death and sexuality." On this occasion I was still under the influence of a piece of news which had reached me a few weeks before while I was making a brief stay at *Trafoi*. A patient over whom I had taken a great deal of trouble had put an end to his life on account of an incurable sexual disorder. I know for certain that this melancholy event and everything related to it was not recalled to my conscious memory during my journey to Herzegovina. But the similarity between "Trafoi" and "Boltraffio" forces me to assume that this reminiscence, in spite of my attention being deliberately diverted from it, was brought into operation in me at the time [of the conversation].[57]

Let us note in passing that example of overdetermination, for it is impossible to understand Freud's position on the explanation of dreams as well as on that of jokes, lapses, etc., if that point is neglected. Boltraffio had been chosen as a replacement name because it was available, just like Signorelli, as the name of an Italian painter of the same period, but also because it contained *Trafoi*—a superficial or insignificant association, it will be said, but one of those mentioned in *The Interpretation of Dreams* as hiding another association, more rational and, as we shall see, often more complex. Furthermore, it had been chosen for the syllable *Bo* (*Bo*snia).

> It is no longer possible for me to take the forgetting of the name *Signorelli* as a chance event. I am forced to recognize the influence of a *motive* in the process. It was a motive which caused me to interrupt myself while recounting what was in my mind (concerning the customs of the Turks, etc.), and it was a motive which further influenced me so that I debarred the thoughts connected with them, the thoughts which led to the news at Trafoi, from becoming conscious in my mind. I wanted, therefore, to forget something; I had *repressed* something.[58]

Thus, the name of the Italian painter, associated with some repressed ideas of death and sexuality, had been carried away into the unconscious with them. Naturally, ideas of death and sexuality did not have that effect by themselves. Freud had not forgotten the subject of the frescoes, nor the Four Last Things of which death is one, nor the Turkish attitudes toward sex: repression was not involved there (it was tied to the news received at Trafoi).

That passage from *The Psychopathology of Everyday Life* had appeared as a paper in 1898. In that paper the same statement was made as in *The Interpretation of Dreams*, which had not yet appeared:

> In the same manner as here and by means of similar superficial associations, a repressed train of thought takes possession in neuroses of an innocent recent impression and draws it down with itself into repression. The same mechanism which causes the substitute names "Botticelli" and "Boltraffio" to emerge from "Signorelli" (a substitution by means of intermediate or compromise ideas) also governs the formation of obsessional thoughts and paranoic paramnesias.[59]

On the question of screen memories, interesting for the way in which it shows the fecundity of the work done on dreams, Freud had not, as we know, gone back to the 1899 paper which included his best example, taken from his own analysis. The "catharsis" method and the first forms of psychoanalysis encouraged the growth of great interest in the exploration of the most distant memories. But the laws of conservation of early childhood memories that were revealed were surprising: important and striking events often left no trace, while other memories of astonishing insignificance were not only remembered but seemed to have been imprinted with particular sharpness, and presented themselves with that "ultra-clarity" which was the sign of a displacement, as Freud had learned from experience. What was displaced, was, as it were, the importance itself, in the form of "psychical intensity" (the first form of the investment theory). That phenomenon had escaped psychologists because consciousness is able to recognize something of that kind only at the price of mistaking it for an error in judgment or a displacement intended to produce witty effects.

> The assertion that a psychical intensity can be displaced from one presentation (which is then abandoned) on to another (which thenceforward plays the psychological part of the former one) is as bewildering to us as certain features of Greek mythology—as, for instance, when the gods are said to clothe someone with beauty as though it were with a veil, whereas *we* think only of a face transfigured by a change of expression.[60]

Freud presented the readers with the screen memory that he had had to explain in his own analysis—but as if it had come from another person, a cultivated man who was interested in psychoanalysis, although his own profession was quite different, and exempt from neurosis "or only very slightly neurotic." The memory unfolded exactly like a dream.

> I see a rectangular, rather steeply sloping piece of meadow-land, green and thickly grown; in the green there are a great number of yellow flowers—evidently common dandelions. At the top end of the meadow there is a cottage and in front of the cottage door two women are standing chatting busily, a

peasant-woman with a handkerchief on her head and
a children's nurse. Three children are playing in the
grass. One of them is myself (between the ages of
two and three); the two others are my boy cousin,
who is a year older than me, and his sister, who is
almost exactly the same age as I am. We are picking
the yellow flowers and each of us is holding a bunch
of flowers we have already picked. The little girl
has the best bunch; and, as though by mutual agreement, we—the two boys—fall on her and snatch
away her flowers. She runs up the meadow in tears
and as a consolation the peasant-woman gives her a
big piece of black bread. Hardly have we seen this
than we throw the flowers away, hurry to the cot-
tage and ask to be given some bread too. And we are
in fact given some; the peasant-woman cuts the loaf
with a long knife. In my memory the bread tastes
quite delicious—and at that point the scene breaks
off.[61]

The analysis of that memory was conducted like
those in *The Interpretation of Dreams*, with a result that
may seem to us unexpected but would not surprise us
if it concerned a dream. The displacement was not made,
as we would expect, from a repressed childhood memory
to a later one. On the contrary, much later fantasies,
dating from adolescence, had been projected into the past
under the form of a memory. One cannot then avoid a
question: Is it pure fantasy, and is that memory an illusion? Or has the memory nonetheless a real basis, and is
it used by the fantasy to express itself?

Analysis tells us that the "cousin" (who in reality
is the niece Pauline) matches another image from adolescence (Gisela Fluss). The force of the displacement,
the desire, is made up of yearnings relating to a love

which could have been possible, and to the choice of another profession (the daily bread). Two distinct fantasies have combined. One relates to the love marriage (with Gisela), and the other to the reasonable marriage (throw away the flowers and come back to the childhood scene where Pauline figured). That was an allusion to the trip to Manchester in 1875.

The yellow color of the flowers permitted the dating of the fantasy: Gisela, now married, wore a yellow dress when Freud saw her again. But it was another yellow, like that of wallflowers or of certain flowers at high altitudes. From these associations Freud boldly inferred that this fantasy came during one of his excursions in the mountains during his adolescence. Whatever psychical "intensity" the daydream had possessed had been displaced on the flowers.

Whether or not that memory goes back to a real childhood event is not very important. (Because fantasy does not record all the elements, Freud tends to concede that it is a memory, based on real events in the past.) Nevertheless there is significance in the fact that a tableau, constructed as in a dream, and in which the repressed desire plays a role, should go back to childhood.

Superstition

The year 1907 had a particular significance for Freud. A superstitious fear, founded as we know on Fliess's numerical calculations which designated that year as that of his death, was to be lifted. It was after 1907 that he made many of his additions on superstition to *The Psychopathology of Everyday Life*.

Freud's attitude toward these matters was "scientific." He stated that superstitious beliefs existed and that psychoanalysis was in a position to explain them. However, that is not a complete summing up of his attitude. Freud spoke of superstition in such a way that it was evident he was analyzing his own attitude. And we know from his letters that although he never abandoned his rational approach, he nevertheless succumbed rather easily to emotions founded on superstitious ideas. In the discussion of these questions in 1907 he used formulas such as "If *I* were superstitious, I would say that . . ." and we understand well what this means: "The superstitious part of myself which I easily combat is ready to think that . . ." As early as 1882, in a letter to Martha, he showed the ingenious way he was, so to speak, able to yield to superstition and fight it at the same time:

> Now I have a tragically serious question for you. Answer me on your honor and conscience whether at eleven o'clock last Thursday you happened to be less fond of me, or more than usually annoyed with me, or perhaps even "untrue" to me—as the song has it. Why this tasteless ceremonious conjuration? Because I have a good opportunity to put an end to a superstition. At the moment in question my ring broke where the pearl is set in. I have to admit that my heart did not sink, I was not seized with forebodings that our engagement would come to no good end, no dark suspicion that you were just at the moment occupied in tearing my image from your heart. A sensitive man would have felt all that, but my only thought was that the ring would have to be repaired and that such accidents are hardly to be avoided.[62]

In spite of whatever humor or good spirits he put into this letter, it is certain that one will view it differently in the light of his paper on "Negation," published forty-three years later. Freud could not be content with a hypocritical solution. To recognize the existence of superstitious tendencies was apparently the preliminary condition for their analysis. In 1907 they were explained as the projection of unrecognized hostile tendencies on the external world. What the superstitious person naïvely interpreted as belonging to the order of external events was explained as an unconscious motivation.

Freud's superstitious attitude was not accompanied by credulity. Jung, who had a weakness for occult beliefs, tried during the period of their closest friendship to shake his rationalism on that point, but without success. By recognizing superstition as part of the human psychical condition, by refusing to deny it, Freud analyzed it and thus kept himself from yielding to it.

Determinism

This question was completely clarified in 1907 with the analysis of the "Rat Man," and it was also to be encountered in later editions of *The Psychopathology of Everyday Life*. In 1901, the conclusion Freud offered in the theoretical chapter of *Psychopathology* was that all the analyzed examples implied a determinism that rules conscious and unconscious life absolutely. The unconscious, for example, shows a "somnambulistic certainty" in the calculations it makes without help from consciousness, so much so that it is impossible to choose a number "by chance." Analysis showed that the choice is not free but is unconsciously determined.

This theory of determinism was not fully developed. It was enough for Freud that it could be shown that the acts we attribute to chance or free will are in fact obeying unconscious mechanisms. He sidestepped metaphysical difficulties which did not interest him. To believe in determinism is to believe basically that everything is subject to interpretation. In analytic practice, such a principle is clearly indispensable.

Many people, as is well known, contest the assumption of complete psychical determinism by appealing to a special feeling of conviction that there is a free will. This feeling of conviction exists; and it does not give way before a belief in determinism. Like every normal feeling it must have something to warrant it. But so far as I can observe, it does not manifest itself in the great and important decisions of the will: on these occasions the feeling that we have is rather one of psychical compulsion, and we are glad to invoke it on our behalf. ("Here I stand: I can do no other.") [as Luther said before the Diet] On the other hand, it is precisely with regard to the unimportant, indifferent decisions that we would like to claim that we could just as well have acted otherwise: that we have acted of our free—and unmotivated—will. According to our analyses it is not necessary to dispute the right to the feeling of conviction of having a free will. If the distinction between conscious and unconscious motivation is taken into account, our feeling of conviction informs us that conscious motivation does not extend to all our motor decisions. *De minimis non curat lex*. But what is thus left free by the one side receives its motivation from the other side, from the unconscious; and in this way determination in the psychical sphere is still carried out without any gap.[63]

This position has nothing philosophical about it. If I consciously make a calculation, I do not have the power of choice over the numbers that I must put down, and if I pretend to choose a number "by chance" I do not have the choice either, because the unconscious calculates better, and the law of the unconscious itself does not neglect any "minimal things." Freud was not interested in the philosophical question of knowing whether it was his freedom that Luther manifested before the Diet. Luther's decision was surely not due to chance; it was either justifiable or analyzable. That is simply what Freud meant in this text by psychical determinism. Chance exists in the material world, where one can play heads or tails. But it does not exist in the psychical world, where one cannot play heads or tails while dreaming. It would be a rigged game, and the moves would be determined by the unconscious.

From 1898 to 1905, everything that concerned Freud pertained directly or indirectly to the functioning of the "psychical apparatus." He explored the intuition that had revealed to him the secret of dreams. He wrote the case of Dora in 1901 but did not publish it; he may have foreseen that the case would cause a scandal. He had perhaps not yet decided to "raise Acheron." However, he treated patients and always kept the therapeutic applications of his ideas in sight. Psychoanalysis had ceased to be "the study of hysteria" and became the theory of psychical functioning in general.

As for the development of the "analytic movement" before 1905, only its prehistory can be guessed at. (History begins for us in 1906 with the minutes kept by the little society in Vienna.) By contrast, the development of theory had definitely gone beyond the initial period. After

1901, Freud did not publish anything for three years. He had a solid base with the dream theory. He was approaching fifty.

In 1905, three important works appeared. One went almost unnoticed while the two others immediately caused a tremendous scandal. The opposition, which was definitely to lift him out of obscurity, did not surprise Freud. It is evident from reading the first pages of Dora's analysis that he regarded it as inevitable. His certainty about the value of his contribution gave him the confidence he needed to confront such a situation. Above all, his theory itself permitted him to foresee and interpret the reactions of the public; he saw them materialize as if they were symptoms. A discovery that touches the unconscious of the reader cannot but provoke resistance. Not only was it impossible to avoid such opposition, but it would have been dishonest.

In any event, his opponents did not raise scientific objections. Naturally, they invoked "science," but only because in their eyes it was a model of chaste thought, and they accused Freud of having concealed scandalous merchandise beneath this honorable standard.

It was with a certain disdain or even contempt that Freud wrote, *before these events,* in the case of Dora:

> The less repellent of the so-called sexual perversions are very widely diffused among the whole population, as every one knows except medical writers upon the subject. Or, I should rather say, they know it too; only they take care to forget it at the moment when they take up their pens to write about it.[64]

One finds here an echo of Freud's experiences with Breuer and Chrobak, and of the remark he once made that those who are the most indignant at hearing sexuality discussed in scientific terms are also the most eager to carry on bawdy conversations as soon as they stop talking "scientifically."

It would be unwise to believe that we have changed all that. There has been a change in which psychoanalysis has undoubtedly played a role, but which might have happened without it: the attitude of puritanical prudery which ruled during part of the nineteenth century is no longer anything but a curiosity of the history of mores. And Freud is no longer condemned in the name of morality. But if in the beginning Freud perceived in contemporary prohibitions of social origin the cause of individual sufferings, he would soon realize that they are implied in our human condition. In any case, since it is impossible for an approach to the knowledge of the unconscious to be made without meeting resistance—as is seen every day in analysis—it simply manifests itself in another way. No one any longer says indignantly, "No, *I* don't have an unconscious like Freud's!" But transposing the opportunities offered by traditional psychology, which gave each man the right to judge as he pleased according to "his conscience," one states, "*All* I know is the unconscious." And thus a personal decision is made and credited to one's own unconscious. Analysis may be fashionable, but the unconscious is always the Unconscious. In any case, Freud was so certain of the impossibility of avoiding public resistance that when one of his books was accepted without criticism he thought he must have gone astray.

CHAPTER FOUR

From Hysteria to a General Theory

FREUD WROTE AN ACCOUNT
of the treatment of an eighteen-year-old girl whom he
named "Dora." The analysis had taken place in 1900, and
the case was ready for publication in 1901 under the fully
justified title of "Dream and Hysteria." It did not appear
until 1905, under another title, "Fragment of the Analysis of a Hysteria." Although the case was a therapeutic
failure, naturally admitted as such, that analysis brought
Freud great satisfaction because it confirmed on all points
the discoveries made in *The Interpretation of Dreams*.
But in confirming what had been acquired, the analysis
was also looking toward the future because the final failure demanded that it be understood. It posed new questions to which Freud had only embryonic answers as
yet. It must be noted that what opened up new avenues
was the extreme scrupulousness with which he adhered
to the theoretical positions already taken. They may not
have been completely sufficient, but there was no question
of abandoning them. And furthermore, it is in this text
that he pointed out that he had not renounced the trauma

86

theory: "I have gone beyond that theory, but I have not abandoned it; that is to say, I do not today consider the theory incorrect, but incomplete."[65] On the other hand, he declared that he had completely abandoned the theory of hypnoid states, but that this was Breuer's and not his. We can only follow his example, and not reject what seems to us to have been left behind today. This is not out of concern for historical or sentimental fidelity to the stages through which Freud passed, but because it is thus that the doctrine was constructed and because it *remains constructed* that way. In any case, it is remarkable that his paper on Dora can be criticized or completed only with Freudian ideas. There is no viewpoint outside psychoanalysis from which it could be commented upon.

In his preliminary remarks, Freud explained his way of writing an observation of this kind:

I will now describe the way in which I have overcome the *technical* difficulties of drawing up the report of this case history. The difficulties are very considerable when the physician has to conduct six or eight psychotherapeutic treatments of the sort in a day, and cannot make notes during the actual session with the patient for fear of shaking the patient's confidence and of disturbing his own view of the material under observation. Indeed, I have not yet succeeded in solving the problem of how to record for publication the history of a treatment of long duration. As regards the present case, two circumstances have come to my assistance. In the first place the treatment did not last for more than three months; and in the second place the material which elucidated the case was grouped around two dreams (one related in the middle of the treatment and one at the end). The wording of these dreams was re-

corded immediately after the session, and they thus
afforded a secure point of attachment for the chain
of interpretations and recollections which proceeded
from them. The case history itself was only com-
mitted to writing from memory after the treatment
was at an end, but while my recollection of the case
was still fresh and was heightened by my interest in
its publication. Thus the record is not absolutely—
phonographically—exact, but it can claim to possess
a high degree of trustworthiness.[66]

We know that in order to deal with the writing of much
longer case histories Freud was to use a slightly different
method: he took notes at night after the last patient
had gone.

As for the therapeutic technique that he utilized in
1900, Freud told us only that it had greatly changed
since the "cathartic method." He let the patient choose
the subject of each daily session instead of trying to
liquidate symptoms one by one. Thus, what related to the
same symptoms could appear in several parts, in different
contexts, and at moments more or less separated by time.
But in Dora's case it was the dreams (there were two of
them) which were, as we have seen, the cornerstones—
taking, so to speak, the place occupied by symptoms in
Breuer's day.

Outside of the analysis of the two dreams, conducted
as in *The Interpretation of Dreams*, and with the omission
of the introduction and the postscript, which were either
added to or completed for the 1905 edition, the text gives
a "clinical frame" wherein the history of Dora and her
"illness" are presented. In it we see that Freud had treated
Dora's father and that he had brought her to Freud "in
order to make her see reason." But it was apparent, and

from the beginning, that the difficulties that were going to hamper the cure were already determined—and precisely by the action of the transference. Dora had complained of having been treated like a barter object in her father's intrigues. He was still treating her as an object when he asked Freud to make her less troublesome for him. And probably the transference of the father to Freud played some role when he brought his daughter to him as his own complaint . . . One can easily see that the father was the principal author of the troubles in the family; Dora also pretended to "make him see reason," and under that pretext added considerably to the existing disorder.

In his postscript Freud regretted not having been sufficiently aware of transference and homosexuality. However, in a way he had paid attention to it. But he was still influenced by Fliess's concept of bisexuality, and he still held the view of transference as applied to the study of dreams and screen memories—the displacement of "psychical intensity" from one representation to another under the effect of the unconscious desire. We see it clearly in the analysis of the first dream. As smoke is mentioned, and Freud was a heavy smoker, and as he liked to repeat, "No smoke without fire," he tried by that means to place himself in Dora's transference and thus missed the other more pertinent signs.

It is evident that the first dream, which was a recurrent one, dated from before the analysis. The point has some importance for the transference theory as indicating whether Dora was bringing a fantasy to the analysis, like a scenario written in advance with a role to be played by whatever actor she could find for it.

We know how cold-bloodedly and deliberately she decided to terminate the analysis. Only in 1914 could

Freud give the theoretical explanation for that kind of action. In 1900 he was still too close to dream meta-psychology, and his explanation was based on somnambulism. The "topical regression," which was to open the door of hallucination to wish representation, had failed; psychical energy then reached the other extremity of the "psychical apparatus," that which rules motility. Dora acted out her scenario instead of analyzing it.

It must be understood that by sticking so narrowly to his theory, after the elucidation of the mechanism of dreams, Freud was using the only means at his disposal to categorize new obscurities with maximum clarity. Because of that, the case displays a quality of truth which still makes it absorbing reading. There is no lack of other and more recent case histories where the gaps present in Dora's have been filled. However, they do not always provoke as much interest or stimulate as much reflection.

Freud the Sexologist

In the introduction to the report on Dora's analysis, Freud did not conceal that he had talked about sexual matters with her. He explained that he was not teaching his patients anything they did not already know. Otherwise, he "called a spade a spade," called organs by their scientific names, and believed that by proceeding in this way he conducted himself with more honesty and decency than was generally found in conversations where these matters were dealt with by equivocal allusions. (Analytically speaking, equivocation reveals the presence and effects of the primary process and of desire.) On the other hand, Dora was particularly well informed for a girl of her age and especially for one of her time, although she did not want to reveal the origin of that information. The whole business could only appear scandalous to outsiders.

But even this scandal was surpassed by that provoked by the publication of *Three Essays on the Theory of Sexuality*. It was deplorable enough that an eighteen-year-old girl was not treated as a model of purity, but *Three Essays* attacked the "innocence" of young children, dealt with their sexual drives, and described these as being the origin of all adult perversions. Of all Freud's books, this was certainly the one to raise the most protest.

In discovering the insufficiency of the trauma theory and the importance of the world of fantasy, Freud felt that he risked grasping the shadow instead of the substance. With *Three Essays* he moved away somewhat from the line he had been following.

His major instrument of discovery had been interpretation; *Three Essays* gave it a subsidiary place. The book as a whole could be compared to what the terminal theoretical chapters had been in his preceding works—chapters in which he drew conclusions from the interpreted examples which made up the other chapters. Now he drew conclusions from his preceding works when they touched on sexuality. At the same time, he had changed his orientation: he was no longer directed toward the world of desire and fantasy. The Oedipus complex was not even named in *Three Essays* (it would be added in the later editions, but only in a short footnote). Desire *(Wunsch)* was not mentioned. Thus it can be said that psychoanalysis was built on two distinct and almost independent or, in any case, very different foundations: *The Interpretation of Dreams* and *Three Essays on the Theory of Sexuality*.

Their destiny has been quite different. *The Interpre-*

tation of Dreams remains a work to be constantly rediscovered, ever new because it opens the door to the unconscious; incomprehension and repression still represent
dangers, but it teaches us how to orient ourselves in the
inexhaustible jungle of fantasy. *Three Essays* has lost the
power to surprise, the power that it initially had. Freud
very quickly became aware of that, since in his preface
to the second edition (1909) he expressed the hope that
his work would "age rapidly" and that all the new concepts it had presented would "become matters of fact."
It can be said that that has been accomplished, at least
for the essentials, but perhaps not without some misunderstanding. A certain way of understanding—of poorly understanding—*Three Essays* gave rise, especially in child
psychotherapy, to a tendency to relate certain neurotic
disturbances to the effects of inhibited *development* and
thus to dream of the chimera of "normalizing development."

The discovery of infantile sexuality obliged Freud
to modify the ideas themselves and to distinguish sexual
from genital.

> The detaching of sexuality from the genitals has the
> advantage of allowing us to bring the sexual activities
> of children and of perverts into the same scope as
> those of normal adults. The sexual activities of chil-
> dren have hitherto been entirely neglected and
> though those of perverts have been recognized it
> has been with moral indignation and without under-
> standing.[67]

Sexology had existed before Freud rebuilt it from its
foundations. The works of Krafft-Ebing, Havelock Ellis,
and a few others had appeared at the beginning of the

century, but they hardly did more than list and classify pathological manifestations. One owes to them, for example, such terms as "masochism" and "sadism." This sexology did not challenge the existence of a sexual *instinct*, defined by its finality or, in other words, conceived of as a *natural pattern* of adaptation. That was necessary so that "aberrations" could be defined. The fact that these aberrations were considered perversions of the "sexual instinct" should have been sufficient, it would seem, to make one suspect that morality and nature were being unduly mixed.

Freud punctured that notion of instinct. The sexual drive *(Trieb)* he posited instead has neither natural object nor natural goal. Normal sexuality has to develop from several component drives, each of which represents what would be a perversion if it should escape normalization, as happens when sexuality in an adult remains fixated at or regresses to one of the earlier stages or organizations it has to pass through.

The text of *Three Essays* was greatly enriched in the course of successive editions. In 1905, Freud utilized only the concepts of component drives, fixation, regression, and sublimation. As often happened in the progress of the development of his thought, his first construction was so correct that later he was able to add to it such concepts as identification, the prevalence of the phallus (that is, castration), pregenital organization, and "sexual theories" of children without having to alter greatly his first text. He almost gave the impression of having foreseen and reserved as early as 1905 the places to be held by these later additions.

The revolution he brought about in this field by his substitution of the concept of drive *(Trieb)* for that of instinct *(Instinkt)* meant the dissolution of a then dominant illusion. The portent of that illusion tended not only to transform obscurities into monstrosities, but also to divide the image of man according to an old metaphysics, preserved for its ethical meaning, as partly animalistic and partly rational.

By relying on analysis of adults and not on observation of children, Freud was able to analyze the stages through which the development of sexuality passes. In later editions these stages became the modes of sexual organization, and soon these modes could be related to the "theories" of children themselves—which gives them a certain flexibility compared to anatomical concepts (the theory of erogenous zones, derived from Charcot's theory of hysterogenous zones) which had first served as the basis to explain the component drives and their transformations.

Amnesia, which blankets the early childhood memories, renders adults incapable of seeing childhood as it is, unless through analysis they triumph over the resistances which protect them from that knowledge. "If mankind had been able to learn from a direct observation of children," wrote Freud in the preface to the fourth edition, "these three essays could have remained unwritten."[68] It serves no purpose to point out that correct observation of children is possible today, even if it must be limited to cases where they are themselves subjects of analysis. For that fact only came about through Freud's discoveries, and it was *necessary* that those be made in the analysis of adults, even if their results could subsequently be verified in that of children.

Component drives are never completely blended in a "normal" outcome. There is always a *residue*. That residue is made up of "perverse" impulses, but that does not determine what it will become. It can become, or rather remain in the state of perversion, but it can also be at the origin of neurotic symptoms and also give birth to "reaction formations" (disgust, shame, morality) which are created at its expense and are made of the same cloth. These reaction formations are the basis of sublimation.

What is it that goes to the making of these constructions which are so important for the growth of a civilized and normal individual? They probably emerge at the cost of the infantile sexual impulses themselves [whose] energy is diverted, wholly or in great part, from their sexual use and directed to other ends. . . . Historians of civilization appear to be at one in assuming that powerful components are acquired for every kind of cultural achievement by this diversion of sexual instinctual forces from sexual aims and their direction to new ones—a process which deserves the name of "sublimation."[69]

Thus, the pressure from perverse impulses, owing to sublimation, increases "psychical effectiveness." It is also the origin of artistic acumen and of character formation. "The multifariously perverse sexual disposition of children can accordingly be regarded as the source of a number of our virtues."[70] Virtues thus have the same origin as symptoms, and it is not impossible that they present themselves in a neurosis as symptoms. It is, in fact, the same perverse residue that supplies the neurotic symptoms.

Thus symptoms are formed in part at the cost of *abnormal* sexuality; *neuroses are, so to say, the negative of perversions.* . . . In any fairly marked case of psychoneurosis it is unusual for only a single one of these perverse instincts to be developed. We usually find a considerable number and as a rule traces of them all. The degree of development of each particular instinct is, however, independent of that of the others.[71]

If one wonders how Freud could have had a certain weakness for Darwin's point of view, it is here that one of the answers can be found. He believed that the theories of struggle for survival and natural selection were superficial, but not the way in which Darwin had eliminated biological finality. As a result, *a higher principle of perfection was no longer necessary.* The greatest human qualities were made of the same cloth as the vices.

His readers did not agree with him. They believed that man was virtuous from birth, which proved his noble origin, and came to be corrupted by society; or that nature was evil and that man through some "supernatural" element escaped it, but not that he derived his virtues from that corrupt nature. Besides, a certain image of the child supported their idealistic mythology; by taking away that support Freud deeply wounded their narcissism. Even today, it is the persistence of the tendency to idealize that makes the acceptance of the notion of sublimation difficult. It is a notion that is hard to theorize about. But in itself, it is simple and deals with the most easily observable facts.

There are many contributions in *Three Essays*, but what is essential is that it is the book of the *Trieb*, or drive, just as *The Interpretation of Dreams* is that of *Wunsch*, or desire. *Wunsch* and *Trieb* are almost always presented by Freud as if on two separate stages; works that contain one of these words do not contain the other. This is almost an unbroken rule, the rare exceptions seeming to be due to carelessness—except once, in the papers on metapsychology, when Freud supposes that the pre-conscious transforms a drive into desire.

These two terms are not easy to translate. *Trieb* should not be rendered as "instinct," for it is in no way a preadaptation to reality, as animal instinct is supposed to be. Furthermore, Freud sometimes uses the term *Instinkt* in precisely that sense—that is, in contradistinction to *Trieb*.* *Wunsch* can be translated as "wish," but as what is meant is not exactly fantasy or illusion, "desire" is a better translation. Desire is related to regret and to a lost object.

Wit

Jokes and Their Relation to the Unconscious was written at the same time as *Three Essays*. Freud kept both manuscripts on two adjoining tables, and relaxed from one by working on the other.

The theories expounded in *Jokes* are fairly easy to master, but they were very original and alien to the mainstream of thought of the period and their importance was not noticed. Their presentation runs through all the detours and doubts that characterize research, which may

---

* In the *Standard Edition of the Psychological Works of Sigmund Freud*, the word *Trieb* is translated as "instinct," as it is in other English translations of Freud's works. The editors explain why, and carefully point out the passages where Freud used the word *Instinkt* in a different sense. In the present work, which is translated from the French, misunderstanding could result if the meanings implied by *désir and pulsion* (the French translations of *Wunsch* and *Trieb*) were lost.

However, in all quotations from Freud's works, which are taken from the *Standard Edition*, the translations "instinct" and "wish" for *Trieb* and *Wunsch* have been retained.

make them more difficult to grasp completely. It appears that once again Freud was using a method inherited from Charcot: to examine a collection of examples long enough to disentangle types, which in turn allows for an interpretation of rough and hybrid forms. It was the method of the natural sciences to which interpretation was added. But that method led the reader to imagine too quickly that he understood the subject matter. Also, Freud had a personal liking for these examples—especially for Jewish stories, of which he had made an anthology for his own use—which may have led him to multiply them needlessly in such a way that his book has often been taken for a collection of amusing stories and his theory for a commentary, which then took second place.

From the first example, borrowed from Heine, we seem to understand everything. The jolly chiropodist Hyacinthe tells Heine that one day he found himself seated quite close to Baron Rothschild, and "He treated me," he said, "in a very famillionaire fashion." The word *famillionaire* is structured according to a technique we know from the analysis of dreams: that of condensation, which belongs to the primary process. The verbal elements are condensed, owing to the presence of the same syllable (*mil*) in the words *family* and *millionaire*. At the same time, the play on words suggests a "thought," a sense, easily understood. That sense, perhaps slightly ironic or satiric, remains interesting without the play on words, but there is no longer anything witty about it. Freud takes the trouble to analyze that meaning in depth. By using Heine's biography, he shows us how the poet represented a whole aspect of his person and his conflicts in the character of Hyacinthe, and how he expressed himself in the words he attributed to him. But the *interest* we find in it is different from the *pleasure* given by wit.

Thus there is no wit unless there is a play on words. That remark is not an answer (it would be one for a pure linguist), it is the statement of a question: How is that possible?

Let us clearly pose the terms of the question. A normal sentence has been subjected to the "syntax" of the primary process, in this example, to condensation. The process *"transferred"* itself, as Freud put it at that time, onto the verbal elements themselves. We are not surprised, after what dreams have taught us. But a certain type of *pleasure* resulted from it, without our being able to speak of the satisfaction of drive or the fulfillment of a desire. Where does it come from?

From that example and from many others, Freud formulated two theses which have not yet lost their power to upset accepted ideas.

One states that the pleasure given by a play on words comes essentially from the fact that it means a return to the power and freedom children have, according to the laws of the primary process, to play with words without any concern for their meaning.

It is true that not all witticisms require such plays on words. Freud, using the vocabulary of the philosophy of his time, then says that the play deals with "concepts" (or we might say that logic is being tampered with). There also, it is not the quality of the thought that gives pleasure but once again the intervention of the primary process—here, it is a question of displacement—which produces the same effect even if it does not deal with verbal elements. There again, the pleasure evokes the freedoms of childhood.

An adult cannot savor this innocent pleasure because an obstacle, the critical faculty—linked to the secondary process—stands in its way, unless there is added to this play of nonsense at least an appearance of meaning. This will divert the attention of the critical sense from the pleasure given by play of infantile origin; otherwise, the pleasure will be denied. We have, if not the proof, at least an indication of the accuracy of this explanation in the fact that the person who is laughing at a joke is not capable of distinguishing whether his pleasure comes from the play on words or from the meaning he finds in it. Both these elements are necessary.

In real *nonsense*, which represents an extreme case,

> the one view, which only takes the wording into account, regards it as nonsense; the other view, following the hints that are given, passes through the hearer's unconscious and finds an excellent sense in it. . . . We can merely decide whether we choose to call such productions, which have freed themselves from one of the most essential characteristics of jokes, "bad" jokes or not jokes at all.[72]

It must be understood that what is refused is not the epithet but the *pleasure*, which falls under the blows of a critical sense which has not been disarmed by the proper technique.

It is not with that technique, entrusted with the protection of pleasure, that the second thesis deals, but with the nature of pleasure. It is explained by the principle of constancy, namely by the discharge of tensions. An energy quota (the energy with which we defend ourselves against the primary processes) has become useless and is freely discharged. At least that is the way it is with innocent, not tendentious, witticisms to which a pleasure of another kind is not added and which only bring about the elimination of tensions between the two processes. Freud's first readers probably had a more "dramatic" idea of the tensions and inhibitions involved, which prevented their glimpsing them in the simple "words just for fun," which is what witticisms are. Thus, an important part of Freud's teaching escaped them.

But these two theses did not resolve the question. Pleasure itself is greater than that which results from the lifting of an inhibition, and each of the two parts (words and "thought") seem to add up to more than each could supply alone; there is a plus value, a "bonus" of pleasure. In other words, the two pleasures do not add up, they multiply. Freud thus confirms Fechner's empirical remark on "the intensification of simultaneous pleasures": we know only the sum total; the factors escape consciousness.

There is a certain kinship between this study and *The Psychopathology of Everyday Life*. After all, wit and lapses obey the same laws. But the aim of the two works is different. In *Jokes* Freud deals with a question of "economy" and seeks to explain the production of pleasure. In *Psychopathology*, psychical determinism, the right to interpret and the necessity of not neglecting any detail, had to be demonstrated.

The study of wit opens up perspectives on aesthetics. Freud always denied that he was interested in problems of pure aesthetics, and it is true that an explanation of aesthetics cannot be found in his work. But by showing us how witticisms function, he gave a possible basis for such an explanation. Wit is not a symptom (although it is similar to it), it is an expedient device (within limits, it has its own *ars poetica*); and like the work of art, it respects defenses as much as it deceives them. One may not go far astray in looking for agreeable or disagreeable "thoughts" in a literary work that pretends to pass them off with the help of form, but it may be a gross mistake to try to explain its aesthetic value by the value of these thoughts, for they may only have been the additional means that art sometimes needs to hide its play on "form." (It is also true that the play on "form" sometimes serves to get across a too daring idea.)

An aesthetics that satisfied itself with unmasking that game would fall into the trap of infantile naïveté since, as we have seen, that game must be masked. We all know it, all of us having been children.

When Freud's son Martin was nine years old he wrote a humorous poem in which the play on verbal material overshadowed the meaning. Being traditional in his tastes, as we know, Freud objected, and Martin explained: "When I do that it's like making faces." (On March 24, 1898, Freud reported these words to Fliess.) Someone who drew the highest human virtues out of the remnants of our perverse drives would certainly not hesitate to justify the highest artistic creations by the necessity to hide the infantile pleasure of making "faces" of that kind. In any case, the book ends with the idea that a certain technique is needed to make us accept pleasure of infantile origin when we are no longer children; when we were children, we had no need of it.

The mode of dream formation (condensation and displacement "transferred" to verbal elements) is not the only model to which aesthetics can refer. There was also a somewhat embarrassing question of "topicality" for Freud to clarify. The dream unfolds on *another stage* (Fechnerian) which cannot be situated in the sphere of the "psychical apparatus." That scene, which is like another world, welcomes fantasy and daydreaming as well and even better than dream hallucination. One is tempted to say that the primary process puts its mark on dream, wit, and poetry, but that there is yet another way for the wish to act within the sphere of the secondary process: here we meet the problem of fantasy.

> The realm of imagination was seen to be a "reservation" made during the painful transition from the pleasure principle to the reality principle in order to provide a substitute for instinctual satisfactions which had to be given up in real life. The artist, like the neurotic, had withdrawn from an unsatisfying reality into this world of imagination; but, unlike the neurotic, he knew how to find a way back from it and once more to get a firm foothold in reality. His creations, works of art, were the imaginary satisfactions of unconscious wishes, just as dreams are; and like them they were in the nature of compromises, since they too were forced to avoid any open conflict with the forces of repression. But they differed from the asocial, narcissistic products of dreaming in that they were calculated to arouse sympathetic interest in other people and were able to evoke and to satisfy the same unconscious wishful impulses in them too.[73]

On such a basis an aesthetics can certainly not be established, for psychoanalysis has nothing to say on the value that can be granted or refused a work according to the criteria in use, these criteria being outside its competence. In the domain reserved for fantasy there is room for works of art, as well as for errors and naïvetés, and Freud always refused to approach those questions. (He said, "We know so little about it!")

He ascribed no artistic attributes to himself. He did

not enjoy modern painting. To Pfister, who wanted to interest him in some expressionist painters then in vogue, he wrote: "For I think you ought to know that in actual life I am terribly intolerant of cranks, so that I see only the harmful side of them and that so far as these 'artists' are concerned I am almost one of those whom at the outset you castigate as philistines and lowbrows."[74] Supposedly, he detested music, but his son Ernst told me that that is an exaggeration, for Freud liked Mozart very much and used to hum some of his melodies when he believed himself to be alone.

We also know that Freudian theories have had some influence on literary and artistic movements, on the surrealist movement for example. But Freud rather tended to disavow that influence and to treat as illegitimate the conclusions drawn from his writings.

In the domain of literature, where considerable ability cannot be denied him, he gave first place to the content, viewing literary art merely as the arsenal of means which permitted the enhancement of that content. Although he was a revolutionary, he clearly appeared as a conservative, a paradox which is explained by the fact that a theoretician is not subject to taste or fashion in the same way as the artist.

In 1907 he published a paper in which he compared literary creation and daydreaming (he would sum it up in a 1913 article in *Scientia*), and in the same year he gave a detailed analysis of a literary text. On close examination, one finds neither aesthetics nor literature involved in these studies. He dealt with artistic creation as another avenue toward knowledge of the unconscious (which neither the artist nor his public care about). Artists do not *know* the things they teach to analysts any more than do dreamers. Shakespeare had no need to know anything about the Oedipus complex in order to enable Freud to discover it. Thus Freud's researches in this field must not be judged from the point of view of aesthetics or of literary criticism.

Gradiva

The novel Freud analyzed in 1907 did not teach him anything about the unconscious that he did not already know. What was confirmed is that nothing escapes psychical determinism, and that the literary fantasy can be analyzed in the same way as a dream, a daydream, or a slip of the tongue. This gave us a brilliant exposition of analytic knowledge already acquired. In a letter to Jung on May 26 of that year Freud said about his literary analysis: "It doesn't contain anything new for us, but it allows us to enjoy [the contemplations of] our wealth."

Jung had brought to his attention a novel by Jensen, *Gradiva*, and it was in honor of their newly formed friendship that Freud wrote an elegant analysis of it.

There were two Jensens. Both wrote novels. Both were alive in 1907, and except for the spelling they had the same first name. Both had completed medical studies. One was Danish and the other, who was German, was born in Holstein in 1837, to further complicate matters. It is the latter, who died in 1911, who was the author of *Gradiva*. (It would appear that Ernest Jones was mistaken about this.) The novel depicts a young archaeologist (we would call him obsessional and fetishistic) who was not conscious of the interest he had in a young girl, his childhood companion. He displaced that interest onto a bas-relief which actually exists (in the Vatican Museum) and which he imagined represented a young girl who

had died in Pompeii. By chance he meets his childhood
companion in Pompeii and takes her for a hallucination
or a ghost. She undertakes to "cure" him by means that
would resemble analysis, if a delusion could be corrected
by an appeal to reality. Such a subject passionately interested Freud, especially because it combined research into
unconscious feelings and archaeological excavations. He
undertook to analyze the dreams and the hallucinations
of the young hero as if he were dealing with a real
person.

From this resulted a convincing and pleasant dem-
onstration of the state of analysis in 1907. It is owing to
Freud that Jensen's novel has not been forgotten; besides,
it can still be quite agreeable to read that old-fashioned
idyll. The naïveté that harms the literary value of the
work accounts for the ease with which it can be interpreted. The art Jensen lacked was the art of defending
and disguising himself.

Of course, the defense was situated somewhere else;
if he confessed his fantasies so easily it was because he
had no knowledge of them. In that period it was natural
that one would want, really with the same naïveté,
to question Jensen himself in the hope of learning more.
Of course, Jensen *had never thought of that.* He even
went so far as to suppose that the meeting of his ideas
with Freud's resulted from the fact that some fifty years
before he had studied medicine!

Moses

Freud revealed his attitude toward works of art in a self-
portrait which was probably the more sincere because
it was anonymous. It is at the beginning of "The Moses

of Michelangelo," which Freud originally published in
1914 without using his name.

> I may say at once that I am no connoisseur in art,
> but simply a layman. I have often observed that the
> subject-matter of works of art has a stronger attrac-
> tion for me than their formal and technical quali-
> ties, though to the artist their value lies first and
> foremost in these latter. I am unable rightly to
> appreciate many of the methods used and the effects
> obtained in art. . . . Nevertheless, works of art do
> exercise a powerful effect on me, especially those of
> literature and sculpture, less often of painting. This
> has occasioned me, when I have been contemplating
> such things, to spend a long time before them trying
> to apprehend them in my own way, i.e., to explain
> to myself what their effect is due to. Wherever I
> cannot do this, as for instance with music, I am almost
> incapable of obtaining any pleasure. Some rational-
> istic, or perhaps analytic, turn of mind in me rebels
> against being moved by a thing without knowing
> why I am thus affected and what it is that affects
> me.[75]

(The last "perhaps" is there for the sake of anonymity.)

That study, dealing with Michelangelo's statue, has
somewhat confused commentators. With a piety which
Freud's memory does not need, they have often hesitated
to recognize how greatly disappointing that essay is.
Several hours a day for several weeks Freud remained
before "Moses," as if—applying Charcot's advice—he
were waiting for the statue "to speak." And he informs
us of his thoughts only as they were concerned with the
sole problem: In what action, in what series of movements, could the pose given to the statue by Michelangelo

fit? Before Freud, most of the critics had seen it as the moment when the prophet is about to rise indignantly and rush toward the worshippers of the Golden Calf. Freud discovered that, on the contrary, having started to move in that direction Moses controlled himself and sat down again; the danger to the precious tablets of the Law restrained him.

We know that Freud was fascinated by the figure of Moses. We also know that he saw himself in a similar position; at that time, he was facing the threat of dissension and dissidence and was asking himself what decision he should take for the future of psychoanalysis (symbolized by the tablets). It may be that he projected his decision in the way he saw the statue, or, which may be the same thing, that he studied the statue as an oracle. But if Freud analyzed himself in front of Michelangelo's work, as he had done not long ago before that of Sophocles, he hid it from us this time. What he let us see takes on the appearance of resistance; he gives the impression of having masked, through an objective study of the work, a question that greatly concerned him and that he did not want to be known.

Obviously, Freud was not blind on this point, but he would have risked blinding us if, on the other hand, he had not brought us precious clarification by giving us an example of how art criticism can aim at serving our resistances by deceiving us on some secondary problems. Art needs similar defenses, and, as Freud showed us in relation to wit, the artist captures our attention on one point to make us more perceptive on another. But the critic does not always know how to play that game.

Jung

Since 1902, and at first unknown to Freud, a professor of psychiatry in Zurich, Eugen Bleuler, had become interested in his ideas, and had undertaken to apply them to the treatment of schizophrenics. Bleuler's assistant, C. G. Jung, was enthusiastic about psychoanalysis—he had "verified" it in its applications to experimental psychology. As soon as he learned of these developments, Freud saw in them, above all, the beginnings of an international recognition to which he then attached even greater importance because he no longer hoped to be recognized in Vienna. Furthermore, the Swiss scientific milieu was Christian; Freud had always believed that anti-Semitic opposition reinforced the resistance that psychoanalysis inevitably raised. He did not worry about the risks of distortion that his doctrine could be exposed to; recognition came first. Later, when the clear-sighted Abraham began to sense and point out the danger, Freud answered him:

> But I think that we as Jews, if we wish to join in, must develop a bit of masochism, be ready to suffer some wrong. Otherwise there is no hitting it off. Rest assured that, if my name were Oberhuber, in spite of everything my innovations would have met with far less resistance.[76]

In fact, Bleuler had not really adopted Freud's ideas, he had utilized them along with others. But Jung seemed to be completely won over and Freud placed the greatest hopes in him. As soon as the project of founding an

international society was born, he thought Jung ought
to be its president. That choice, however, drew rather
violent objections from the Viennese analysts.

It is known that the project turned out badly. Although Freud had been, in the beginning, very tolerant
of the first doctrinal deviations, in 1913 he took the
trouble to clarify his own position in opposition to that
of Jung, and out of that concern came a great number
of extremely important developments.

The temporary adhesion of the Zurich school had
several lasting results. First of all, something of it remained on the level of international recognition; and then
it brought Freud valuable followers such as A. A. Brill,
Oskar Pfister, and above all, Karl Abraham, a young Berlin psychiatrist who had worked in Zurich. But if the
Zurich school played a role in extending psychoanalysis
to the study of psychosis, it was hardly through Jung or
Bleuler, but through Abraham, and especially through his
pupil Melanie Klein.

As Abraham had been the first to understand, the
break with Jung was unavoidable; an emotional rivalry
made impossible the reconciliation of doctrinal disagree-
ments. However, from these quarrels Freud retained
some grudge toward those of his entourage who had
shown a certain tendency to keep analysis for themselves
alone. He recognized the very great value of Abraham,
but he did not completely trust him. Much later, he
would admit the rightness of Abraham's past judgments,
but without wanting to listen to new advice relating to
other difficulties. "But should you turn out to be right
this time too, nothing would prevent me from once
again admitting it," he wrote on November 6, 1925; but
he did not have time to admit it, for that was his last

letter before the death of Abraham. Freud thus remains with a sort of unpaid debt against his account.

Little Hans

In 1908, Freud was still very conciliatory. Far from criticizing Jung's contributions, he fused them with his own ideas (that would be especially apparent in the analysis of the "Rat Man"). As for the analysis of little Hans, it contained nothing that could agree with Jung's theses, rather the contrary. It was in the analysis of childhood that Freud would later seek his best arguments to refute Jung.

In *Three Essays*, Freud denied that anything could be gained from the direct observation of young children. But it was understood that once the problem was clarified through the analysis of neurotic adults, it became possible to verify the "reconstitutions" through the study of children themselves. Likewise, Freud—anxious to bring direct proof of what he had asserted in *Three Essays*—undertook to ask among the friends and students around him that observations on the sexual life of children be gathered.

He knew Hans's parents. He had analyzed the mother (a hysteric) before her marriage; the father had attended his lectures, and Freud had received information about their child long before the question of his analysis came up. When the little boy (he was five years old) showed phobic symptoms, it was decided to undertake the analysis.

The role of analyst was entrusted to the father, Freud being convinced that *nobody else could have taken that role*. We know that that conviction weighed heavily on the history of child analysis. Even today, the place of the parents in such an analysis remains a subject of controversy. One can only speculate on what that history would have been if Freud had personally undertaken Hans's analysis. The father reported on the analysis to Freud, who directed it while remaining well in the background; we may believe that he wanted to be involved as little as possible, so that it would result in "impartial" testimony as to the correctness of the theses from *Three Essays*. We almost have the proof that such was his aim in the fact that in the *Jahrbuch*, where this study appeared for the first time, it was given as *presented* by Freud and not as his work, to the surprise of commentators.

As was customary, that analysis perfectly confirmed knowledge already acquired and opened up new questions that created an obligation to go beyond that knowledge. (Children had their theories on sexuality; the Oedipus complex was accompanied by fantasies relating to castration; a phallic phase had to be introduced in the series of organizations, etc.) All that would only be completely clarified some fifteen years later.

In order to understand these developments, it is necessary to distinguish the text of the 1905 edition of *Three Essays* from the later revised editions. Eventually, in 1922, the 1908 analysis would have a surprising sequel which would justify, and perhaps impose, modifications on a major point: the manner of conceiving the relations between the conscious and the unconscious.

But what first interested Freud was the confirmation which that study gave to discoveries already made. In 1918, when he explained the way he had analyzed the infantile neurosis of the "Wolf Man" (retrospectively, as he had always done, obtaining knowledge of infantile sexuality in the course of analysis of an adult), he invoked the direct analysis of children as proof of his statement. If he did not need that proof himself, it was nonetheless a powerful argument against his opponents, particularly Jung.

> In any case it may be maintained that analysis of children's neuroses can claim to possess a specially high theoretical interest. . . . the essence of the neurosis springs to the eyes with unmistakable distinctness. In the present phase of the battle which is raging round psycho-analysis the resistance to its findings has, as we know, taken on a new form. People were content formerly to dispute the reality of the facts which are asserted by analysis; and for this purpose the best technique seemed to be to avoid examining them. That procedure appears to be slowly exhausting itself; and people are now adopting another plan—of recognizing the facts, but of eliminating, by means of twisted interpretations, the consequences that follow from them. . . . The study of children's neuroses exposes the complete inadequacy of these shallow or high-handed attempts at reinterpretation.[77]

In 1908, Freud did not have to defend himself against "reinterpretations" but against the incredulity of those who had read *Three Essays*.

Besides that point, Hans's analysis, of course, dealt with the phobia theory. A third point, which today is still a subject of discussion, concerns the role that psychoanalysis can play in the theoretical and practical problems of child education.

In 1922, Hans—who was no longer "little" but a strapping nineteen-year-old—paid Freud an unexpected visit. Freud was pleased to see that he was perfectly normal, contrary to the fears of his opponents.

> One piece of information given me by little Hans struck me as particularly remarkable; nor do I venture to give any explanation of it. When he read his case history, he told me, the whole of it came to him as something unknown; he did not recognize himself. . . .[78]

That does not seem extraordinary to us. Although analyses are often forgotten, they nevertheless have their effect. But Freud, in the exposition itself, had explained the cure process by the passing of what was repressed into *consciousness;* he had even thought of attributing to consciousness a *biological* function (in other words, adaptation). He was not the sort of man to let the contradiction imposed by Hans go unnoticed. The value (biological or not) of the "passing into consciousness" would no longer be taken for granted and would subsequently be questioned.

In the 1923 edition of the case history, Freud added a note at the bottom of page 3 of the introduction, in small type, where he substituted "preconscious" for "conscious," and from September 1922 on (Hans had visited him in the spring) he started to develop a new topical conception capable of explaining the particularly remarkable fact that Hans had just told him. This gives us an idea of the way Freud elaborated and corrected his theoretical constructions. Undoubtedly, it was not this experience which itself was at the origin of the new topical concept of 1923, but it seems to have triggered it.

The "Rat Man"

The analysis of the "Rat Man" ("Notes upon a Case of Obsessional Neurosis," 1909) marks the end result and the conclusion of the whole period we have just reviewed, going back to the abandonment of the "Project" of 1895 and to the experience of transference with Fliess. Now, finally, the contents of Chapter 7 of *The Interpretation of Dreams*, *The Psychopathology of Everyday Life*, *Jokes and Their Relation to the Unconscious*, and *Three Essays on the Theory of Sexuality*, all of them, came together and fitted.

It was in October 1907 that a twenty-nine-year-old Viennese lawyer came to Freud. The young man had returned to Vienna after being on maneuvers as a reservist, during which time, as a result of relatively minor incidents, he had fallen into the state of anxiety and disorientation that made him seek Freud's help. He knew of him through one of his books (*The Psychopathology of Everyday Life*), in which he had recognized the similarity between descriptions of psychical mechanisms and those whose existence he had observed in himself. That was in itself a trait of obsessional neurosis and the mark of the "secondary" character of those psychical mechanisms. A hysteric would not have recognized himself so easily in reading a study of his psychological mechanisms.

Freud treated this patient for a little less than a year, after which he considered him cured—regretting that he thereby lost the opportunity of continuing further study of the case. On the other hand, as the young man was to die in the war of 1914-1918, the success or failure of the cure could not be followed as far as with Anna O., the "Wolf Man," or little Hans.

Although this analysis confirmed the discoveries in *The Interpretation of Dreams* more clearly than any preceding analysis, dreams only play a secondary role; it is the whole neurosis which appears to be one long dream. Freud would remark on this a little later.

In the case of the "Rat Man," as in dreams, something of the unconscious triumphs over repression in order to express itself in a language which remains incomprehensible to the patient just as does the manifest content of dreams, and which must be interpreted the same way. In other words, the patient is protected from his own truth by *secondary* defenses which do not belong to the unconscious as such and yet escape from becoming conscious. At that time Freud had not yet defined the exact nature of the unconscious as such, and in 1907 he encountered a paradox that would remain unresolved until the "Wolf Man" analysis.

When Freud represented obsessional neurosis as a dialect of the language of hysteria, he used a metaphor to designate a type in a class. But that metaphor was not chosen by accident. The "Rat Man's" neurosis clearly expressed itself in its own dialect, which created difficult problems of translation. The case history could very properly be considered selected writings in a dialect to be interpreted. The *Traumdeutung* was already a collection of that kind, as was Dora's analysis. But the latter, strictly limiting itself to the text of the dreams, still did not give the technique all the dimensions it received in the "Rat Man's" case.

The latter's unconscious (let us remember it was not yet the Ucs.) was formed in large part from *remembered words*, oracles, broken promises, debts which could not be repaid, and verbal slips. In addition, it was also necessary to take into account events and speech which antedated his birth (for example, that his father had never been able to pay off his debt, had betrayed his true love in order to marry a rich woman, had considered suicide, etc.). All this constituted the structure of the patient's fate, the myth which kept him captive and the origin of his neurotic repetitions. Although unconscious, it all had its place in the secondary process; what was discovered concerning the primary process was a *death wish*, the moving force of the entire neurosis.

The analytic transference, which had remained so blurred in Dora's case, would be the transference of that death wish onto the analyst, and it is through this device that the unconscious desire would be activated and the cure made possible. It can be observed how confidently Freud conducted himself in this situation. A confidence, however, that he never mentioned, though it was obvious in the text and in the original record. So far as defenses and secondary material were concerned, his technique consisted of inexorably pursuing his patient and breaking down all of his defenses with a determination contradicting the famed benevolent neutrality; but, on the other hand, where the primary process was concerned he demonstrated complete reserve and patience. This is how he obtained the transference of the unconscious desire, the only means of effecting the cure.

An analyst today realizes there are still many things missing in that 1907 analysis: pregenital organizations, homosexuality, castration, superego, among others. But if one tries to add them to the case it becomes apparent they can only be used as labels which pointlessly identify what has already been expressed or implied. For example, what good is the notion of the superego when the pa-

ternal oracles, familial myths, and unconscious promises
expose its anatomy to us with a clarity generally lost in
this type of case history if they are buried under the
vague and general concept of the superego.

While Freud was preparing this case history he was
still under Jung's influence. This can be deduced from
the role he assigns to "association complexes" where
images are grouped according to the laws of Jungian
symbolism. Freud himself used the idea of the *Passwort*,
which deals with the way in which one word links itself
to another, as *Ratte* (rat) to *Rate* (quota) or to *ver-
heiraten* (to marry). When he goes along with Jung's
concepts anything can associate itself with anything else
—for example, *rat* can be associated with *syphilis*. However, seeing the way Freud conducted his analysis, one
can be sure that the influence of the Jungian ideas remained marginal and superficial.

It is not known how it happened that Freud, who
systematically destroyed his rough drafts, kept the original notes of this analysis among his papers, where they
were found after his death. The reader of these notes
risks being disappointed when he discovers how much
the definitive text conforms to them. (That disappoint-
ment deserves to be analyzed: what did the reader then
hope to discover?) That conformity shows us how
everything was already organized at each session. It is
unlikely that the patient never spoke irrelevantly, but
Freud did not take down his words as a stenographer
would! Going from the notes to the report he had no
need to sum up, nor to screen, but only to eliminate what
was repetitious; so that when we try to find left-out
details in the notes, we learn nothing which is not in
the text. (Freud wrote his notes at the end of the day,
letting forgetfulness do its work, without being hampered

by the useless abundance of "material" or blind attention to every detail. He never had anything to correct; if something he did not expect surprised him, that was a characteristic of the analysis which would be noted in the final report. No matter how faithfully or not he is followed, in that aspect of his work Freud remains un-equaled.)

However, he probably never fully theorized upon the content of that extraordinarily rich case (on the language, on the way the patient withdrew by referring to himself in indirect speech, and even on the technique). With the "Rat Man" it can be said that psychoanalysis was finally formulated. It would be significantly modi-fied, beginning with the "Wolf Man," the next analysis, in which would be harvested part of what had been sown in the "Rat Man's" case. But all the essential ele-ments were already present, and those unanswered ques-tions which still remained had been posed.

The "Wolf Man"

In Freud's opinion, the "Rat Man" had been cured "too quickly," which had prevented him from pursuing the analysis as far as could have been wished in the interests of science. He would not run up against that "incon-venience" in the analysis he undertook some three years later of a young man who was given the nickname of the "Wolf Man" from the content of a dream which held a central place in that analysis. ("From the History of an Infantile Neurosis," 1918.)

We do not know the whole of that analysis. We only know that it was very difficult, although the patient gave an impression of lucidity *such as is only obtained under hypnosis*, and it indeed seems that there was a psychotic element at work. What Freud tells us is only that part of the analysis dealing with the infantile neurosis which took an obsessional form.

The analysis of that obsessional neurosis, although in some ways less satisfying than that of the "Rat Man" (there is no question of transference in this retrospective analysis and it tells almost nothing of the very important relationship between the patient and his analyst), is much richer. Castration, masochism, homosexuality, identification, and anal eroticism, which were not mentioned in 1907, found their place in it. *Verwerfung*, or foreclusion,* a new form of knowledge rejection distinct from repression, appeared in it.

One of Freud's purposes in writing this account was to refute Jung by showing the presence of libidinal motives and the absence of cultural aspirations in early childhood. A large part was devoted to the question of determining how far the images of the adult subject projected into the past can falsify reconstructions, and even introduce into them the fantasies of the analyst. That was an objection made by Jung. The problem of the relation of fantasy to reality would therefore be posed again, as if one had gone back to 1897, and Freud remarked that the old trauma theory, which after all had been built on the impression created by analytic practice, had returned to the scene again. One must question the authenticity of the facts reported by the patient, utilizing when possible the method of historical criticism to confirm the veracity of the seduction by the sister and of the observation of the parents' sexual relations (*Urszene*, or primal scene).

---

* "Foreclusion" is an Anglicization of *forclusion*, the word by which Jacques Lacan translates Freud's term *Verwerfung*.

*Amalie Freud and
Sigmund in 1867.*

ABOVE:

Freud poses for Marie Bonaparte in his office in Vienna, amid his collections.

BELOW:

Freud informs his patients of his new address. He would remain there until his departure for England.

Docent Dr. Sigm. Freud

beehrt sich anzuzeigen, dass er von Mitte
September 1891 an

IX. Berggasse 19,

wohnen und daselbst von 5 – 7 Uhr (auch
8 – 9 Uhr Früh) ordiniren wird.

WIEN, Datum des Poststempels.

Ernst Brücke (signature)

Vienna's General Hospital.

ABOVE:

*At Worcester, September 1909: (stand-
ing, l. to r.) A. A. Brill, Ernest Jones,
Sandor Ferenczi; (seated, l. to r.) Freud,
Stanley Hall, C. G. Jung.*

BELOW:

*The young Dali charmed Freud during
a visit he paid him in London. He drew
Freud's portrait on a blotter.*

ABOVE:

A corner of Freud's desk.

BELOW:

Diploma of Doctor of Laws Honoris Causa from Clark University, presented to Freud in 1909.

Clark University
Worcester, Massachusetts, U. S. A.

To all to whom these presents may come, Greeting:

Be it known that

Sigmund Freud
has been created

Doctor of Laws
honoris causa

in this University, and is entitled to all the dignities thereunto appertaining.

Given at the City of Worcester, in the Commonwealth of Massachusetts, this tenth day of September in the year of our Lord One Thousand Nine Hundred and Nine.

Witness the Seal of the University, by the hands of the authorized representatives of the Trustees and of the Faculty:

For the Trustees   For the Faculty

ABOVE:

At the 1911 Weimar Congress the following can be recognized: Freud, Otto Rank, Ludwig Binswanger, A. A. Brill, Paul Federn, Karl Abraham, James J. Putnam, Ernest Jones, Eugen Bleuler, C. G. Jung, Lou Andréas Salomé, Sandor Ferenczi.

LEFT:

Pastor Pfister.

ABOVE:

The sculptor Oscar Nemon working on a head of Freud.

BELOW:

The "Committee" in 1920: (seated, l. to r.) Freud, Sandor Ferenczi, Hanns Sachs; (standing, l. to r.) Otto Rank, Karl Abraham, Max Eitingon, Ernest Jones.

Freud knew that the problem did not rest there, that the question of reality was not essential, and that the necessity of refuting Jung did not demand a falling back upon that realistic attitude. Besides, whether or not the fantasies referred to a reality, in either case Jung's position had to be refuted. (However, the need to find real experiences behind the fantasies induced Freud in this account to go so far as to formulate a hypothesis that he was never to abandon, namely, one of species memory, of a *phylogenetic heritage*.)

What he reproached Jung (and Adler) with was, above all, the retention in analysis of only those elements that did not risk provoking resistance because they were acknowledged and recognized before the discovery of analysis, such as actual conflicts or selfish interests.

The views opposed to his

> are usually arrived at on the principle of *pars pro toto*. From a highly composite combination one part of the operative factors is singled out and proclaimed as the truth; and in its favor the other part, together with the whole combination, is then contradicted. If we look a little closer, to see which group of factors it is that has been given the preference, we shall find that it is the one that contains material already known from other sources or what can be most easily related to that material. Thus, Jung picks out actuality and regression, and Adler, egoistic motives.[79]

This method of treating original ideas—and not only Freud's—appears frequently in the history of ideas, and psychoanalysis continues to be exposed to it without Jung or Adler any longer having anything to do with it.

Sublimation

From the time that Freud published *Three Essays* he no longer revealed much information about his personal life; as he himself said, his biography really coincided with the development of his doctrine. It is not simply that most of his correspondence is inaccessible to us; actually, his attitude changed profoundly at that time. He no longer confided to the reader how he dealt with his own resistances. In 1910, the year Freud began the analysis of the "Wolf Man," Sandor Ferenczi complained about the lack of reciprocity in their relationship. He said he confided in Freud but Freud did not confide in him. On October 6, Freud answered:

> You not only noticed, but also understood that I *no longer* have any need to uncover my personality completely, and you correctly traced this back to the traumatic reason for it. Since Fliess's case, with the overcoming of which you recently saw me occupied, that need has been extinguished. A part of homosexual cathexis has been withdrawn and made use of to enlarge my own ego. I have succeeded where the paranoic fails.[80]

What this was about was sublimation. The word first appeared in *Three Essays*, and in 1910 he was working on the new edition. He added only a few notes, keeping important additions for later, but in a study on Leonardo da Vinci and in another on the jurist Schreber he again took up the question of sublimation on the one hand, and its relation to homosexuality and to paranoia on the other.

Leonardo

What interested him about Leonardo were mainly his own concerns. What was the source of that need to know which carried Leonardo so far beyond his contemporaries in the study of nature and the sciences, along paths that no one had thought of taking and that no one thought of following him on? That trait, in part compulsive, made him neglect the art in which he excelled, and often prevented him from truly completing his numerous and diverse undertakings.

The answer was that it had to do with imperfect sublimation. In Leonardo's case a homosexual component going back to his childhood was implicated. The paradox of the study undertaken by Freud was that nothing was known about the painter's childhood—except for the wonderful fabulistic detail of a kite perching on the cradle of the sleeping child and putting its tail between his lips.

On this narrow base Freud built two constructions. One, as he willingly admitted, was purely conjectural, being biographical reconstruction; the other, extremely sound, was an outline of the theory of drives, which would only be fully developed in 1915, in his work on the drives and their vicissitudes.

The origin of the epistemological drive (the need to know) lies in the curiosity of the child confronted by the enigma of sexuality. That drive can follow three paths, have three "destinies": (1) It can remain inhibited, in which case intelligence stops developing and the outcome is stupidity, mental retardation. (2) It can develop in the form of intellectual activity but fail to detach itself from its first object and therefore remain *sexualized*.

Intellectual work, consequently, will bring with it the pleasures, anxieties, guilt, and perversions proper to the sexual sphere. Research will continue, but its results will not have the value they ought to have. Such is the case in obsessional neurosis, for example. (3) The drive can be sublimated (detach itself from its sexual object), and curiosity operate freely in the service of authentic intellectual interests. Freud noted, first in *Three Essays* and again in 1908, that the most perverse elements of sexuality are the ones most likely to facilitate sublimation. Leonardo da Vinci had undoubtedly sublimated his sexual curiosity, but his life showed that he had inhibited part of it.

This study contained many other things. For the first time, an outline of the theory of narcissism was sketched. (It is also found in a seemingly later note in *Three Essays*.) Freud also took up again and refined a view on the relationship of religion and neuroses which he would develop later.

It would be a mistake to look in that study for anything to do with painting or the origin of Leonardo's talent. It was Pfister, not Freud, who discovered a vulture in the "Saint Anne" painting in the Louvre; it takes a certain naïveté to believe that that vision explains anything. On the other hand, commentators (especially the English, who are knowledgeable in matters of ornithology) were disturbed by the fact that Freud—victim of an error of German translators—had put a vulture in place of the more common kite. He also indulged in mythological considerations which crumble once that error is corrected. Obviously, the importance and interest of this work are not along these lines.

One sometimes comes across readers who believe that Freud undertook this study because he discovered a vulture in the "Saint Anne" painting. These are interesting and typical displays of resistance; Pfister's discovery was already the product of an analogous resistance, which recalls the one Freud had exhibited—in fact *proposed to us*—in front of Michelangelo's "Moses." In front of Leonardo (more than in front of his paintings) he did not let himself be distracted from what touched him most intimately. (The letter to Ferenczi proves it and at the same time explains why he does not confide in the reader.) Pfister's naïve "discovery" may have encouraged other naïve persons—although they may not have needed encouragement—to look for hidden images in works of art. However, long before, Henry James's "The Figure in the Carpet" had wittily mocked that type of resistance, without recognizing what it was, of course.

Schreber

Basically, Freud was pursuing the same line of research with the Leonardo study as he was with the study of the memoirs of Schreber. Indeed, it could be said that there is a fourth path along which sexual curiosity may get lost: paranoid psychosis. (There is even a fifth, where the epistemological drive, sublimated and desexualized, again turns secondarily to sexual curiosity and permits that "aggrandizement of the self" briefly mentioned in Freud's reply to Ferenczi: it is psychoanalysis itself. It is certain that Freud was asking himself that kind of question in 1910, but, as he said at the time and in the same letter, he no longer needed to reveal himself.)

In 1903, Daniel Paul Schreber, the presiding judge of an appellate court, following a long psychiatric confinement very skillfully conducted and won a lawsuit by which he obtained his freedom and the right to publish the book in which he related his own mental illness. He nevertheless remained insane. In a note to a passage where he learnedly discusses a legal point—namely, under what conditions a person can be confined against his will—he simultaneously regards himself as a harmless mental patient who is said to be prey to hallucinations, and asserts his own conviction that his so-called hallucinations contain objective truths unrecognizable by other people. In effect, he has obtained from the court the right to be insane without hurting anyone.

His delusion depicted a fantastic cosmology, a universe where his own destiny was to be transformed into a woman by higher powers in order to give birth to a new humanity in a destroyed world. His "cure" consisted in the acceptance of that destiny, after a grandiose and impotent struggle.

Schreber's moral and intellectual qualities, his memory, his lucidity, his complete sincerity, make of his book the most perfect account of a paranoic in the literature. It is unobtainable in German, but there is an English translation, and a French one is being prepared. Outside of specialist circles, it could be of some interest for its literary qualities.

Regarding Schreber, Freud offered a formulation of the varieties of paranoiac insanity, starting with denied homosexuality. The sentence that states the homosexual position: "I, a man, love him, a man," can be negated: "I do not love him, I hate him." But the second proposition can be reversed: "I do not hate him, he hates me." The persecution mania is now present. Another transformation leads to: "It is not him I love, but her," from which "It is she who loves me" leads to erotomania. Maniacal jealousy is founded on: "It is not I who love a man, it is she." There remains one more possibility:

"I do not love anyone at all," which is the basis of megalomania.

This game of combinations gives an almost mechanical account of all "positions," but not of the formation of symptoms. These are explained by the "silent" withdrawal of libidinous investment from the external world, which produces the feeling of the end of the world and the necessity of rebuilding it. That work of reconstruction is manifested "noisily," and that is what we see in the form of insanity. What has been abolished internally now comes back from the external world in the form of hallucinations. (In Lacanian terms, that which has been foreclosed on the Symbolic level manifests itself on the Real level.)

But there is another aspect to be considered.

Thus in the case of Schreber we find ourselves once again on the familiar ground of the father-complex. The patient's struggle with Fleschig [the psychiatrist who had treated him] became revealed to him as a conflict with God, and we must therefore construe it as an infantile conflict with the father whom he loved; the details of that conflict (of which we know nothing) are what determined the content of his delusions. None of the material which in other cases of the sort is brought to light by analysis is absent in the present one: every element is hinted at in one way or another. In infantile experiences such as this the father appears as an interferer with the satisfaction which the child is trying to obtain; this is usually of an auto-erotic character, though at a later date it is often replaced in phantasy by some other satisfaction of a less inglorious kind. In the final stage of Schreber's delusion a magnificent victory was scored by the infantile sexual urge; for voluptuousness became God-fearing, and God Himself (his father) never tired of demanding it from him. His father's most dreaded threat, castration, actually provided the material for his wishful phantasy (at first resisted but later accepted) of being transformed into a woman.[81]

Thus, psychoanalysis approaches a case of that type from three different sides and supplies three convergent though quite distinct explanations.

In a 1912 postscript, Freud noted that Jung must have had good reasons for affirming that humanity's mythopoeic forces have not been extinguished. He must have found some satisfaction in recognizing it in relation to an insanity which, in its form, clearly does not differ from some mystical experiences.

CHAPTER FIVE

Incest and Parricide

Long before there was any question of psychoanalysis, Freud was inclined to find an antibiological character in civilization. It was a banality, but he was struck by it. On August 29, 1883, after attending a performance of *Carmen* (that opera was then eight years old), he wrote these "bourgeois" thoughts to Martha:

> ... the mob gives vent to its appetites, and we deprive ourselves. We deprive ourselves in order to maintain our integrity, we economize in our health, our capacity for enjoyment, our emotions; we save ourselves for something, not knowing for what.[82]

In this appears, in embryo, the idea of opposing the reality principle to the pleasure principle, but perhaps also the idea that that opposition is not as explicit as a hedonist might believe. The paradoxes of obsessional neurosis, the mysteries of the feelings of guilt, probably required another principle. Why does man deny himself pleasure? The Epicurean solution (denial is the means of obtaining greater satisfaction) is surely not sufficient. There are prohibitions which do not come from such self-seeking calculations and which nevertheless must rest on something other than religious myths. These are in effect "the reflections of our inner psyche,"[83] and it was therefore necessary that the prohibition be first a psychical reality. The model of all prohibitions is that of incest; it has that impenetrable clarity that marks true imperatives and that resembles the absurd.

It seemed to Freud that natural man—a pure biological fiction—ought to be "the savage without inhibitions" for whom the two prohibitions of the Oedipus complex (incest and parricide) had no meaning. Diderot also had that idea, but since then anthropology has shown us only "primitives" even more tied up than we are in inexplicable taboos and totemic inhibitions stricter than the imperatives of culture. (Sir James Frazer's *Totemism and Exogamy* appeared in 1910.) Besides, clarifying the question of the origin of religions might have provoked a break with Jung; that would not have displeased Freud, provided he had not directly taken the initiative for the break.

Nevertheless, the real reason that obliged him to consider these questions was that he kept stumbling on what was to become the problem of the superego. The judgments of moral conscience have an obscure foundation, to be looked for in the area of the unconscious. They impose themselves without need for explanation or justification. In this they are identical to the taboos that "primitive" people cannot account for at all, any more than obsessional neurotics can understand their compulsive thoughts.

As a starting point, Freud adopted on faith (and much too quickly), the postulates generally formulated by the social sciences of his time. For example, he uncritically accepted that consanguineous kinship, being "biological," was more natural than other forms of kinship and therefore must have chronologically preceded totemic institutions. Nor did he dispute the idea that made contemporary savages studied by anthropologists equivalent to prehistoric men and also to children erroneously included in the same "primitivism." But as soon as he found himself again on his own ground, when he showed the comparisons to be made between ancient customs and certain traits of obsessional neurosis, he did not follow anyone, and it is here that the soundest part of his contribution is found.

It was not the first time that Freud's work had surpassed the scientific facts on which it was founded. Today's anthropology can easily criticize yesterday's, which is what Freud had to lean on, but that is a matter between anthropologists. The essence—the matter of oedipal prohibitions and the fantastic world that surrounds them—is not damaged by the abandonment or refutation of totemism.

The two so-called totemic prohibitions (not to kill the totem, not to have sexual relations with a partner belonging to the same totem) correspond to the prohibitions of the Oedipus complex. Perhaps their own Oedipus complex has made totemism so popular with anthropologists. Freud, in any case, could not make that ironic rejoinder. He contented himself with noting the universal character of the Oedipus complex which can explain all customs. But was it explainable itself?

Freud tried to give it a historic (prehistoric) foundation and constructed a myth: One day the sons killed the primal father and ate him, and there followed a new social organization founded on guilt. The myth exercised great emotional power over its author. After being very pleased with it, Freud was seized with real panic when the time came to publish it.

The objective truth of the myth has been easily contested. Freud himself admitted that it need not be true, a fantasy serving just as well. One seems to hear here an echo of the questions posed in the analysis of the "Wolf Man," which was taking place at the time. If Freud preferred to believe in objective truth, the reason was surprising: primitive man was not inhibited and therefore had no need to substitute fantasy for action.

There is no need to attack or defend Freud in the matter of proven facts. It remains that the original transgression—mythical or not—the guilt-producing image of the dead father, "the one who did not know that he was dead" (according to the wish of the dreamer), or the one of the "Rat Man," is what the elaborations of *Totem and Taboo* try to settle. That is the end result of the analysis of obsessional neurotics and, with the same stroke, of religious attitudes—and the first approach to a question which would take on increasingly great importance: the question of guilt.

In seeking to establish the foundations of incest prohibition in reality, Freud was neither the first nor the last to give an explanation of that difficult question that rested on a vicious circle. Nevertheless, in about the same period, in 1911, he published a paper in which he took the opposite position. At the beginning of the paper he stated that he was inclined to give more importance to the reality principle, but in the final analysis he gave the major role to fantasy, which is neither the unconscious nor the thought obeying the reality principle. However, in a passage which is essential because it defines the analytic position, Freud shared his concern with us:

> But one must never allow oneself to be misled into applying the standards of reality to repressed psychical structures, and on that account, perhaps, into undervaluing the importance of phantasies in the formation of symptoms on the ground that they are not actualities, or into tracing a neurotic sense of guilt back to some other source because there is no evidence that any actual crime has been committed. One is bound to employ the currency that is in use in the country one is exploring—in our case a neurotic currency.[84]

It is exactly there that Freud gave the example of the dream about the father who "was dead and did not know it"; the only object of the guilt feeling in the dream is the fantasied wish of the dreamer.

Freud thus placed within the "reality" of prehistory what today exists only in the form of fantasy. It is difficult to say whether he intended to utilize thereby the hypothesis of "phylogenetic heritage," or if he simply could conceive only of a mythical explanation for that type of problem. But one thing is clear and certain: if he situated a reality in prehistory, it was certainly not to introduce it into analysis but obviously to keep it out of it. And there is no contradiction—rather the opposite —between *Totem and Taboo*, where he demanded a real fact on which to base guilt, and the paper where he eliminated that hypothesis and insisted that guilt was founded on fantasy.

Narcissism

In 1914 one could believe that Freud had only to polish an already established theory, defend it, or even invent myths to illustrate it. One could not have foreseen that, partly to defend it against Jung, he was going to radically transform the theory of the ego, which was to have all sorts of consequences, eventually even affecting the explanation of guilt, one of his first concerns. He introduced a new concept: narcissism, which he had alluded to earlier. He practically created the word spelled in that way—*Narzismus*. "When I asked him," Ernest Jones reported, "why he did not use the more correct *Narzissismus*, he simply replied that the sound displeased him." Let us remember that he could not stand Sigismund . . .

Primarily, narcissism served the purpose of answering Jung's objections, which were suggested by the study of schizophrenia. Of course, the concept was a necessary one, regardless of Jung. In 1911, Freud was tempted to give a "biological" function to the ego, to make it essentially the agent of adaptation. But he seemed to have given up the idea; in any case, he destroyed the papers he had written along that line. Now the ego became an "object," an *image*, a vestige of past identifications; the ego of narcissism could not coincide with the ego of the inhibition of drives and of the control of motility. Naturally, Freud did not abandon the old conceptions, but he presented an aspect of the ego which was completely unexpected and confusing for the analysts of the period.

Jones vividly relates the confusion of those who until then had understood the theory as a conflict of drives— the ego drives against the sexual drives—and how they tried to preserve the same position by making it into the conflict between the "libido of the ego" and the "libido of the object." (A whole period and perhaps a whole trend of psychoanalysis was to remain marked by these efforts at restoration.) They could not accept the idea that this ego, which in effect succeeded the ancient reason, was also a figure of fantasy, an imaginary object, a mirror of mirages—and the agent of madness at least as much as that of reason. Even today, not everyone has accepted it.

And, indeed, the final push came from madness. It was in order to explain megalomania and hypochondria that the notion of "narcissistic psychoneurosis" became necessary. It is in those "disorders" that investments have been concentrated in the ego of the subject. It is the same with sleep and with organic illness. Falling in love itself occurs as a defense against narcissistic investments when these go beyond a certain level. But it cannot avoid retaining the mark of its origin: the choice of the object is narcissistic when the object represents the subject himself, or what he has been, or what he would like to be, or a part of himself (a child).

> Parental love, which is so moving and at bottom so childish, is nothing but the parents' narcissism born again, which, transformed into object-love, unmistakably reveals its former nature.[85]

In the neuroses the ego, incapable of realizing its ideal, seeks to rediscover a narcissistic position

> by choosing a sexual ideal after the narcissistic type which possesses the excellences to which he cannot attain. This is the cure by love, which he generally prefers to cure by analysis. Indeed, he cannot believe in any other mechanism of cure; he usually brings

expectations of this sort with him to the treatment
and directs them towards the person of the physician.
The patient's incapacity for love, resulting from his
extensive repressions, naturally stands in the way of a
therapeutic plan of this kind. An unintended result
is often met with when, by means of the treatment,
he has been partially freed from his repressions: he
withdraws from further treatment in order to choose
a love-object, leaving his cure to be continued by a
life with someone he loves. We might be satisfied
with this result, if it did not bring with it all the
dangers of a crippling dependence upon his helper
in need.[86]

One can only be impressed by the way Freud treated
the contributions of the libido received by the ego: Whatever their origin, he adds them together. The love from
others is added to the love of self; in effect, we are not
in the sphere of the drives but in that of fantasies and desires, and the status of the libido itself, which is fundamental, does not altogether clearly emerge. It is understandable that those psychoanalysts who had invested
everything in "instinctual dynamics" were thrown off
when it became necessary to superimpose, not to substitute, the new conceptions upon it.

During the first years of World War I, his therapeutic work left Freud with some free time, and he used
it to work out his theoretical concepts. He apparently
intended to construct a complete metapsychology, but
he has left only a few chapters.

Unlike many of his other writings, it was not to be
an attempt to convince the unbelievers. He wanted to
explain systematically the conceptual formulations sup-

porting the entirety of psychoanalysis, intending his book for psychoanalysts and those laymen who already believed. Despite the major modifications made to it a little later, the doctrine expounded in these short chapters represents even today the necessary foundation for everything that can be said to be Freud's in psychoanalysis.

It is therefore necessary to provide, not a résumé—for Freud's chapters are already almost résumés—but an overall view to guide the reader, if he so desires, in the study of these basic texts. As for the reader who does not have the intention of plunging into this difficult area of Freud's work, he has the option of skipping the end of this chapter.

In the kind of dogmatic exposition which Freud's chapters represent—it will be the same in 1933 in *An Outline of Psycho-Analysis*—the starting point is the concept of the drive *(Trieb)*.

Drives not only have no object consigned to them by some "innate" disposition, but they are even susceptible to transformations—the characteristic that differentiates them from animal instincts. These transformations of the drive—reversal into its opposite, and turning around upon the subject's self—must be examined *before* the unconscious and repression are mentioned. Thus they have nothing in common with the mechanism of reaction formations, nor with the facts of ambivalence. Ambivalence applies exclusively to the fusion of love and hate, which are not drives. They are attitudes of the ego and they have their origin in the way in which the ego is created when it separates from the object world. Besides, drives are basically unconscious, whereas hate and love are not.

The second chapter deals with repression, which represents one of the vicissitudes of the drives. (Freud's plan is very easy to follow, in spite of the fact that he

eliminated seven of the chapters he had envisaged and
most certainly written.) Repression, we learn, cannot
affect the drive itself, which is unconscious by nature. It
affects the representation (*Vorstellung:* idea, image)
which is the representative *(Repräsentanz)* of the drive.
That representative is the bearer of a *Besetzung* (cath-
exis), that is to say, of a definite quantity of psychical
energy which is in effect nonmeasurable. This psychical
energy is made up of an impulse material whose overall
name is libido.

The way this energy charge moves from one representative to another determines the fate of each representative and is the specific cause of its repression. (James
Strachey is the one who translated *Besetzung* as "cath-
exis," and at the time Freud raised objections to that translation.)

Regardless of their content, the representatives—
which need only to be identifiable to function—act as
signs even if they present themselves as images, in the
manner of the pictures in a rebus or of hieroglyphs. The
word "sign" being ambiguous, in modern linguistic phrase-
ology let us say they must be regarded as the "signifiers"
and not as the "signified." Lacan's reinterpretation of
Freud's writings employs this evidence as a starting point.

The unconscious, the site of repressions, is the subject
of Freud's next chapter. Years before, in the analysis of
the "Rat Man," Freud had encountered a difficulty: some
elements—not part of the unconscious—still escaped entering consciousness. This difficulty was overcome by
opposing the systematic concept of the *Ucs.* to the descriptive aspect of the unconscious. Beginning with that
distinction Freud would write out the word "unconscious" when there was a question of designating what
escaped the patient's consciousness, and *"Ucs."* when it

pertained to the unconscious as a system or a topical division. In the same way he was to use the abbreviations *Pcs.* and *Cs.* for "preconscious" and "conscious."

What characterizes the psychical process in the *Ucs.* (the primary process) is the extreme mobility of the cathexes, which explains the displacements and condensations first discovered in dream analysis.

In the *Pcs.*, owing to the role played by words, the cathexes are more stable. Freud here took up an idea from Breuer, who had noticed that the bonds of psychic tension were loosened in "hypnoid states." Breuer assumed

> the existence of two different states of cathectic energy in mental life: one in which the energy is tonically "bound" and the other in which it is freely mobile and presses towards discharge. In my opinion this distinction represents the deepest insight we have gained up to the present [1915] into the nature of nervous energy, and I do not know how we can avoid making it.[87]

However, in the *Pcs.* some degree of freedom must subsist, or otherwise there would be no secondary process at all. The representations exchange "a small part" of their investment. Thus speech, logical thought, adaptation to the external world, are possible.

The preconscious had been introduced at first to furnish an explanation for facts such as memory preservation. When it became the *Pcs.* it assumed much greater importance. The *Cs.* system is hard to distinguish from the conscious in the descriptive sense, except when added to the *Pcs.* to become the *Pcs.-Cs.* system. Consequently, the fact (descriptive) that the conscious does or does not perceive a psychical element has little theoretical significance. Among the chapters Freud wrote for his metapsychology was one dealing with the conscious. He destroyed it. One can guess that this was because he couldn't add much to previous statements concerning the *Ucs.* and the *Pcs.*

In dividing the psychical field by boundaries (called censorships), Freud drew its topography. (This refers to the first topography: *Ucs., Pcs., Cs.;* the second topography—id, ego, superego—was to be superimposed on it without replacing it.) His theory of the distribution of the cathexes is called economy, and the examination of the psychical forces yields the *dynamics*. These nearly inseparable three—topography, economy, and dynamics—constitute metapsychology.

In neuroses (which Freud at the time called "transference psychoneuroses" because their investment was transferable to objects) the "return of what has been repressed" is involved. This return takes place in hybrid formations where what is repressed mingles with defenses. Thus symptoms are formed. The model of symptom formation is in the "normal" phenomenon of dreaming.

In psychoses the investment is not transferred but remains attached to the ego. Freud called them "narcissistic psychoneuroses." It follows from the preceding, which was already implied in "Narcissism," that the ego functions like a representation. Many of Freud's successors have not wanted to take this consequence into account, particularly the champions of "ego psychology," who could not resist making the ego an ally of ancient reason. Their justification is that Freud kept two incompatible conceptions of the same ego side by side. Here again it is Lacan who, by distinguishing the ego from the

I, systematically brought out the implications of a theory in which Freud had compared the ego to an image. Furthermore it is by returning to the point where Freud encountered this question that Lacan's theoretical conceptions can be understood.

Contrary to what happens in neuroses, where the interpretation of the "return of what has been repressed" creates difficult problems, one sees in psychoses the direct evidence of the *Ucs.*, particularly in the schizophrenic's language. This observation, which psychiatrists could confirm for themselves, ranked high among the reasons that made them adopt Freudian hypotheses. But for psychoanalysts, and for Freud himself, it only exacted further research.

Freud proposed the following solution. In trying to get well, the schizophrenic attempts to escape from narcissism by transferring the cathexes on the words themselves, which he manipulates according to the laws of the primary process, that is to say, in the way the *Ucs.* functions in normal or neurotic patients. From this, he arrived at the no longer enigmatic formula: In neurosis, it is the cathexes of the *Pcs.* that are withdrawn (it should be added, "to a greater or lesser extent"), whereas in psychosis, it is those of the *Ucs.*

We do not have the chapters, which were certainly written but destroyed, dealing with the conscious and with anxiety. We can easily do without them, for the theory of anxiety was to be radically transformed a little later (with war neuroses as a starting point), while as far as the conscious goes there was little to be said. But another part concerned sublimation, and we must regret its loss. At that point in Freud's plan, a chapter on dreams was to provide a transition. This has been preserved; it contains refinements of points already dealt with in Chapter 7 of *The Interpretation of Dreams.*

One learns here that it is necessary (and difficult) to entrust to the same ego that carries narcissistic investments the power to make the distinction between hallucination and reality. One also discovers a very interesting topographical point: by penetrating in the form of representation into the *Pcs.*, the drive is transformed into desire; that is to say, fantasies are created in the *Pcs.* which topographical regression will make into dreams. In 1912, in a paper written at the request of the Society for Psychical Research, one could already discover the outlines of this viewpoint.

There is no doubt that Freud wanted to make "Mourning and Melancholia" one of the chapters of his metapsychology, which was to end with nosographical examples. But there is no doubt, either, that he did not originally write it with that intention. Except for a letter to Fliess in 1897 he had hardly concerned himself with melancholia. But Abraham, more aware of the problems of psychoses, did consider that subject in a 1911 paper. It was natural that Freud told him about the study he himself was preparing. Abraham, protesting that he did not want to raise any questions of priority, made a few suggestions. Drawing from his clinical experience, as well as from ancient cases of lycanthropy which contained delusionary self-accusations of anthropophagy, he proposed the concept of *incorporation* in place of that of identification. Freud found his ideas useful. In a letter to Abraham on May 4, 1915, he says: "I have unhesitatingly incorporated [!] in my essay what I found useful. The most valuable point was your remark about the oral phase of the libido; the connection you had made between mourning and melancholia was also mentioned."[88]

However, as we will see, he remained faithful to identification.

He adopted Abraham's idea of using mourning as a normal model. Melancholia, like mourning, has as a starting point the loss of the loved object. But that loss does not appear in reality. On the other hand, contrary to what happens in normal mourning, the ego of the melancholiac is divided. One half unmercifully criticizes the other, and the half thus attacked represents the lost object itself through identification. It must be supposed that the love felt for the object had been of a narcissistic nature. The loss of the object seems to provoke the transformation of love into hate.

The conflict between the two halves of the ego resembles mourning and often ends by being displaced by a manic state. In 1915, Freud vainly tried to explain the manic state in terms of investments, but it was not until 1921 in *Group Psychology and the Analysis of the Ego* that he found a more convincing explanation in the fusion of the ego with the superego.

In any case, it is clear that that study on melancholia was one of those which called for major subsequent development.

By approaching the questions of the metapsychological theory, Freud was compelled to examine his epistemological position and the value of his theoretical constructions. He apparently adopted the point of view, then reigning in Vienna, which had been elaborated by Ernst Mach: A theory has no truth; truth is in observations, which theory has only to report in a logical or practical way. However, a more careful examination shows that the Freudian theory cannot in any way be reduced to that neopositivist schema. The theory is not the simple systematization of observations. It remains the theory of interpretations, just as in the study of a foreign language, the theory of the language can result only from its decipherment. This creates epistemological problems far more subtle than those Ernst Mach had dealt with.

CHAPTER SIX

A Drive Toward Death or Destruction Which Works Silently. . . .

Anglo-Saxon analysts, influenced by a biological philosophy founded on the struggle for survival, have found it quite natural to make aggression a reaction to frustration. But in Freud's eyes difficulties could not be explained in this way. Less simplistic views could be found in German philosophy, in Schopenhauer and in Nietzsche, but it is doubtful that they influenced Freud. What decided him was the need to account for, or at least to point out, the paradoxes of masochism, self-reproaches, negative reactions, the universality of guilt feelings in general.

Those preoccupations went back rather far: they could be glimpsed in a 1905 paper on "Psychopathic Characters on the Stage." However, the question would undergo a decisive modification. Here is how it was posed first: How can the representation of suffering be a source of pleasure? Later, the question became: What is the nature of the compulsion to repeat disagreeable situations, as is the case, for example, in traumatic neurosis and in children's play?

When one steers a course between the two great principles of pleasure and reality, the analysis of those repetitions (in life they manifest themselves as a repetition of failures, and during treatment they are found again in transference) leaves a remnant. That remnant is the compulsion and repetition itself, which seems impossible to justify.

A young child, by making some object disappear and reappear in a game, creates a repetition of the unpleasant situation caused by the departure of his mother. That game is a verbal game, the German adverbs *fort* and *da* stressing departures and returns. The purpose is to symbolize a situation or, as Freud said, to bind together excitations arising from the drives, to submit them to the secondary process by means of verbal activity which is at the disposal of the preconscious. If the preconscious fails, it lets the repetition continue indefinitely.

From that, it was inferred (in a very speculative way) that any drive tends to repeat a former state that the subject has been obliged to abandon (this brings it close to being a desire) and through an extrapolation which Freud considered risky—but which he favored—he posited the existence of a "death drive" (*Todestrieb*) which tended to bring back living beings to a state anterior to life (that of inorganic matter). This 1920 thesis was resumed in 1933 in the fourth of the *New Introductory Lectures on Psycho-Analysis,* and there the exposition was easier to follow.

Freud was not convinced that he had demonstrated the existence of a death drive in the biological sense. But he showed how a distinct principle seemed necessary to him to account for repetition, hate, aggression, and guilt. The postulate which had guided him from the start, the quest for pleasure as regulated by reality, that is to say hedonism moderated by wisdom, could not suffice. From the biological viewpoint, the hypothesis of the death drive remains paradoxical or arbitrary, especially if translators make an "instinct" of it. For psychoanalysis, in one form or another, it is indispensable. What is involved is a drive which is of as fundamental a character as the sexual drive, and which would become the other pillar of a structure whose first pillar was the libido; so much so that the ego, already dislodged from its old position of polarity and subjected to narcissistic investments, would furthermore become the object of attacks from this new quarter. It can be seen that the necessity of that development was predictable ever since the introduction of narcissism.

According to Freud, the general purpose of drives was the reconstitution of an anterior state through the application or extension of the principle of constancy. But once released, the death drive, which is the agent of repetition, is the only one left to seek that return to the anterior state. While Eros, or the libido, represents the principle of union, it is not seeking a lost union. If it sometimes seems to be, this is because the death wish blends in silently with the action of the libido. The widely held idea that love resembles a nostalgia is not Freudian. The strongly Freudian concept that the desired object has been substituted for the lost object through the effect of the displacement mechanisms is in itself different. But if it tends to be confused with a nostalgia for the original union, it is as though it were under the influence of the death wish which mingles with it, as poets have always known—or perhaps written without knowing.

If the existence of the death drive has not yet been widely accepted, if it still gives the impression of being a useless paradox, it is because until now no one has dared to write the "three essays on the theory of the death drive" which would go beyond the work of criminology just as the *Three Essays on the Theory of Sexuality* rendered sexology obsolete. It is clear that resistances from that side are infinitely stronger than from the side of libido.

The Ego and the Others

The ego, because it had been dislodged from its old position of polarity, posed new problems. It was not surprising that they should have emerged for the first time at the end of the essay on narcissism. In order to investigate them thoroughly, it was not indispensable to deal with the behavior of crowds; but that question will remain posed as an obscure paradox as long as politicians and policemen, not knowing how to handle responsibility in collective actions, have found no other recourse but to take hostages under the name of "agitators." Gustave Le Bon's *The Psychology of Crowds* (1895) was only descriptive and seems to have been a mixture of political concerns and phobic fears.

In *Group Psychology and the Analysis of the Ego* this question was taken up again and clarified by means of the concepts of identification and of the *ego ideal*. The ego ideal filled the vacuum left by the critical agency. The latter was indeed capable of plunging the subject into a state of guilt, whereas the ego ideal, through identification, permitted him to find again an infantile situation, as does hypnosis. Thus it brought an (irrational) remedy to guilt (Freud could not guess how all this was going to be verified under Hitler). For him it was primarily the opportunity of explaining in a systematic way the different levels of identification, which is the equivalent of distinguishing different levels inside the ego, until it became necessary to detach them from it. His conclusions were not to be clarified until 1923, but the 1921 paper contained many new remarks of great interest, for example a discussion of the relation between hypnosis and infatuation.

The New Topicality

Between 1915 and 1925 Freud had written a large number of papers on technique and especially on metapsychology which must be passed over here because of the impossibility of doing them justice without long explanations. "I realize from my experience with art in miniature that this medium compels the artist to simplify, but the result is often a distorted picture,"[89] he wrote Stefan Zweig on February 7, 1931. That work of simplification has its necessities and its limitations, and the reader who wishes to escape the yoke of that "medium" can only be referred to the texts themselves. Some of them are very important, for example, "Fetishism" and "Negation."

The article on negation cannot be summarized: it is only four pages long. Instead, it should be elaborated upon. The first model of psychical duplicity—metapsychological dualism—which made possible the interpretation of hysterical symptoms, was the opposition of repressed material to consciousness. But the very concept of repression (*Verdrängung*) itself was to be divided, and along with other concepts—foreclusion (*Verwerfung*), repudiation (*Verleugnung*), condemnation, projection, etc.—would partially constitute a list of the forms of defense. Negation (*Verneinung*) must logically be included.

It might also be advisable to add sublimation or reaction formations.

The few critical pages Freud devoted to it are based on a clinical remark. The patient who, in speaking of a female image which appeared in one of his dreams, said, "In any case, I am sure it is *not* my mother," in reality unwillingly confessed that it was she—or, in any case, that he had thought it was she.

Clinical facts caused the abandonment of what from the metapsychological point of view had been freely conceded until then, namely, that after repression was removed the patient continued to defend himself against it through a secondary mechanism of an obsessional type. If the secondary defense is overcome—in other words, if the patient accepts the interpretation of the psychoanalyst —the clinical effects are nevertheless nil. Consequently, no dent has been made in the repression.

What is evident is that the content of a repressed idea—its *lexis*—can penetrate consciousness and be recognized by the patient on condition that it appears in a negative form which respects repression.

This remark is an introduction to the theory of intellectual functioning. Owing to negation, the thought, so to speak, validly liberates itself from the obstacles of repression without liberating from these same obstacles the patient who has formulated the thought.

Freud discussed the connections between that negation of judgment and the attitude of refusal. The latter took over the expulsion mechanisms at work when the ego was constituted—by separating from what displeased it. His conclusion was that the creation of the "negation symbol" had transformed the refusal into negative judgment and therefore was at the origin of the development of thought. Mallarmé, before Freud and probably influenced by Hegel, had discovered the basic role of negation in the development of language. But he placed himself in a completely different perspective.

In "Fetishism," Freud explained the effects of a belief which was repudiated but neither repressed nor denied. He thus introduced a new idea resembling a mode of defense which was probably nonneurotic. The repudiated belief was the one which affirmed the existence of the maternal phallus. That belief seemed to disappear but was still preserved. The existence of fetishists was proof of it; that belief, preserved in darkness, was, however, inaccessible and impossible to overcome. The fetish represents the indelible stigma, the memorial to the discovery of feminine castration and, at the same time, to the conservation of a contrary and hidden belief. The possibility of simultaneously embracing two contrary beliefs, one official and one secret, secret even from the subject himself, does not belong to repression, nor to the mechanism of negation. In order to explain it, an old idea (that of splitting) must be taken up again and perfected to make it into the *splitting of the ego*. At the end of his life, in one of his very last papers, Freud would return to that problem. It is that splitting which explained a quantity of dual and contradictory attitudes. In particular, the idea of life after death, which is found not only in religious beliefs but also in some pathological attitudes where the subject does not deny the death of someone who was dear to him but behaves absolutely as if he or she were still alive.

All the work done on metapsychology led Freud in 1923—in order to avoid certain confusions and to explain feelings of guilt—to construct a new topicality in *The*

of Eros and thenceforward desires to live and to be loved.[90]

The ego, which played a role in the conflict in the beginning, is not even the referee any longer, and it runs the risk of becoming the stakes. Narcissism itself appears as a defense against the death drive. Through this new topicality Freud indicated where difficulties now lay for him and with what attitude he intended to approach them. He did not have to draw very precisely the boundaries of the new additions, and readers who search his texts for the means of drawing them more exactly are sometimes embarrassed.

The formulation of the new topicality was regarded by Freud himself as his last important contribution to analytic theory. His shift of interest was due, he said, to a profound change:

> . . . what might be described as a phase of regressive development. My interest, after making a lifelong *détour* through the natural sciences, medicine and psychotherapy, returned to the cultural problems which had fascinated me long before, when I was a youth scarcely old enough for thinking.[91]

The date of the "new topicality"—1923—was also the date when he discovered he was suffering from cancer. He survived only at the cost of numerous operations and considerable suffering. When he approached his seventy-fifth year, he decided not to restrain himself any longer in any way and, as a first step, started smoking cigars again in unlimited quantities. It can be thought that in 1923 he was already taking a similar liberty in approaching the subjects that attracted him the most.

Happiness is Not the Product of Culture . . .

He had once said that his true interests were of a philosophical nature. That was an improper use of the word. In reality, he had never adopted or accepted the attitude of the philosopher.

> Even when I have moved away from observation, I have carefully avoided any contact with philosophy proper. This avoidance has been greatly facilitated by constitutional incapacity.[92]

It is not difficult to relate some of Freud's concepts to those held by philosophers. However, one can be sure that Freud's concepts do not derive from philosophical writings but only from reflection on clinical facts. Philosophy's goal is wisdom, a substitute for salvation, and the philosopher has no other praxis. Obviously, the praxis of psychoanalysis is of an entirely different order. If Freud moved away from it somewhat, it was in order to seek an application to more general questions in the area of the social sciences and the problems of civilization.

In 1913, shortly after the publication of *Totem and Taboo*, he clearly saw the relation of psychoanalysis to the social sciences.

> For the neuroses themselves have turned out to be attempts to find *individual* solutions for the problems of compensating for unsatisfied wishes, while the institutions seek to provide *social* solutions for these same problems. The recession of the social factor and the predominance of the sexual one turns these neurotic solutions of the psychological problem into

caricatures which are of no service except to help us in explaining such important questions.[93]

That position, which retains some validity, is the opposite of the "culture sociology" since it consists in taking the study of neurotic "solutions" as a model for understanding institutions as being themselves answers to the same questions. Freud would remain faithful to it; but his viewpoint was modified according to the interests that occupied him until the end of his life. The first of these modifications was his criticism of cultural solutions, which, if they are an answer to the same questions, were in his eyes no better than neurotic solutions.

Religion as Illusion

The study of group psychology has shown how a group can maintain itself through identification with a common ideal. A whole society could achieve this through the identification of the lower classes with the ruling classes. But the plurality of ideals, which is always present, maintains conflicts and gives a real outlet to destructive impulses. No just division of the products of labor, no satisfaction of biological needs, no technical improvements in the exploitation of nature (it is to these points that Freud had reduced socialist programs) can bring any remedy. In fact, civilization must subsist on other bases. Among these must be considered religion, along with philosophy, art, and science.

It must be determined what religion has done, and what it would be able to do in the future, for the progress of civilization. It is not primarily necessary to demonstrate that it is an illusion, but rather to decide what role that illusion has played and what role it yet can play.

Religion has been useful in helping to domesticate asocial impulses. But it has not been able to achieve sufficient results. It has not made men more moral, and it has brought them as much anguish as it took away. Truth could do more. For outside of the fact that by itself it is worth more than an illusion, it would also be a better way to improve civilization. Therefore, what Freud opposed to religion was science. It has its weak points: men are less sensitive to its truths than to emotional reasons; it can scarcely resolve all problems. But it is still quite recent compared with religion, and we cannot find elsewhere the answers it does not provide: beyond reason, no other jurisdiction exists. The science Freud was talking about was obviously not only positive science; it was all knowledge that aims only at truth, and psychoanalysis was part of it.

Freud had an imaginary interlocutor voice objections to him:

> Man has imperative needs of another sort, which can never be satisfied by cold science; and it is very strange—indeed, it is the height of inconsistency— that a psychologist who has always insisted on what a minor part is played in human affairs by the intelligence as compared with the life of the instincts— that such a psychologist should now try to rob mankind of a precious wish-fulfilment and should propose to compensate them for it with intellectual nourishment.[94]

But naturally, Freud had no trouble in reminding that somewhat Jungian interlocutor that it was always by means of intelligence and reason that psychoanalysis had approached the irrational aspects of psychic life. Those who might have misunderstood were those who envisioned a rationalist as one who, by using as resistance the appeal he makes to reason, refuses to face those problems. Freud aimed his strongest arguments against religious instruction for young children. When someone, he said, "has once brought himself to accept uncritically all the absurdities that religious doctrines put before him and even to overlook the contradictions between them, we need not be greatly surprised at the weakness of his intellect."[95] Freud himself had had no religious instruction whatsoever. On the surface, he seemed to have regretted it; but after what we have seen, one cannot doubt that he considered himself lucky. Besides, he was simply and clearly an atheist (which was less essential than that he had escaped religious instruction). In 1925 he wrote to the editor of a Zurich Jewish magazine:

. . . I can say that I stand as far apart from the Jewish religion as from all other religions: that is to say, they are of great significance to me as a subject of scientific interest, but I have no part in them emotionally. On the other hand I have always had a strong feeling of solidarity with my fellow-people, and have always encouraged it in my children as well. We have all remained in the Jewish denomination.[96]

To be a Jew was for him a personal and family matter. His letters indicate that he was proud of the qualities shown by other Jews, but that also, on occasion, he enjoyed criticizing their faults. He kept an open mind and remained completely faithful to what he knew himself to be. The few commentators, friendly or hostile, who have attempted to find in psychoanalysis a Jewish inspiration would certainly have been sharply rebuked: a scientific truth cannot be Jewish. In an unfortunate moment it was left to Jung to forget that fact. But undoubtedly, the discovery of psychoanalysis indirectly owes something to the fact that Freud was Jewish. If the rigor of his judgment may have come from his lack of religious instruction, the soundness of his character and his indifference to opposition go back to the "persecutions" he may have suffered as a Jew, even if these persecutions had been relatively moderate.

When, in 1873, I first joined the University, I experienced some appreciable disappointments. Above all, I found that I was expected to feel myself inferior and an alien because I was a Jew. I refused absolutely to do the first of these things. . . . I put up, without much regret, with my non-acceptance into the community; for it seemed to me that in spite of this exclusion an active fellow-worker could not fail to find some nook or cranny in the framework of humanity. These first impressions at the University, however, had one consequence which was afterwards to prove important; for at an early age I was made familiar with the fate of being in the Opposition and of being put under the ban of the "compact majority" [Ibsen's expression]. The foundations were thus laid for a certain degree of independence of judgment.[97]

But it must be understood that the independence thus acquired also freed him of many familial or ethnic traditions. This is evident from the way in which he chose his sons' first names.

CHAPTER SEVEN

The Mystery of Guilt

ALTHOUGH FREUD'S INTER-
est was increasingly drawn toward cultural questions,
he still took the time to write on strictly psychoanalytic
matters. Three great works were written between 1936
and 1938: *An Outline of Psychoanalysis*, a very dogmatic exposition of the entire analytic theory, and two
studies, "Analysis Terminable and Interminable" and
"The Splitting of the Ego in the Process of Defence," in
which he intended to go back over points that remained
unclear. In this he remained faithful to his original concepts, but he now brought very valuable corrections and
precisions to them—for instance, on the role of language
(hence of the *Pcs.*) in the extension of the field of consciousness.

But the question which had occupied him for some
time and would concern him to the end of his life was
of a slightly different nature: the outrage one felt when
confronted by the guilt of the innocent, an issue which
had confronted the world as early as the time of Job.

The two answers that Job got were not satisfactory. One, a naïve happy ending, was that he had been "tempted," in other words subjected to a trial, and that everything was reversible on condition that he resisted temptation. The other, a grandiose mystery, was that he had nothing to do but to repent "in sackcloth and ashes" without asking for an explanation.

Freud's answer was that the man who believed himself innocent was guilty in reality.

He was a criminal by intent; his crime was in fantasy and guilty childhood wishes, for the death drive had demanded and obtained some satisfaction one way or another. Disguised, secret, latent satisfactions were shown through symptoms: guilt is, in a way, one of these symptoms. The already half-neurotic agency of the superego as an accuser, a prosecutor for the other side, probably fills a socially useful function, but that superego is above all principally the agent of the death drive; and the more innocent we become, namely, the more we move away from aggressive impulses, the more the latter pass into the service of the supergo, which is thus better armed to torture us. Hence the most "innocent" carry the heaviest burden of guilt.

The discontents of civilization cannot find their cure in good will, goodness, or the love of others. Those virtues are not the result of a sublimation but of an idealization. At the time of the publication of *Civilization and Its Discontents* (1930) Freud, at William Bullitt's instigation, drew a harsh picture of the misdeeds of idealization in a study on Woodrow Wilson. That merciless analysis hit many prejudices head on, but in a frightening way it illustrated the thesis according to which good cannot be done in the name of illusion.

Before Freud, poets had seen, albeit in a mysterious way, that death and the ideal were partners. It took Freud a long time to discover that the death drive was no less important than the libido, which it closely parallels. In primary narcissism, the libido is almost one with biological forces; but the death drive already occupies the same place. The libido can invest an external object and become sexual desire and love; aggressiveness and hate follow it like shadows. Finally, in secondary narcissism, the libido invests in the ego itself. The death drive attacks the same ego, accuses it, condemns it, tortures it. Freud was astonished that he could have hidden these truths from himself for so many years. That length of time was testimony to the resistance protecting them, and that resistance was a measure of their importance. Civilization is finally founded on the reinforcement of guilt feelings. Freud approved of the efforts of socialists (although he tended to think of them as utopians); but as we have seen they cannot correct what is most important: fate ordains that if they achieve better control over aggressive impulses it shall be at the cost of an increase in the terrible feeling fed by the invincible death drive.

Freud's pessimism might be reminiscent of some religious attitudes. But those attitudes are based on illusion and idealization, which are exactly what he denounced. Biology had taught him that life has neither goal nor significance. To demonstrate this he used an irrefutable argument: "Look at the animals!" However, there was not a trace of skepticism in that. His realism made him envision, as the only possible attitude, the best utilization of guilt, with the help of reason and truth, and the discarding of illusions for the progress of civilization. Illusions, far from being able to help men, are among the symptoms of what is wrong with civilization.

The Murdered Prophet

During the last five years of his life, first in Vienna and then in London, Freud's interest was once more directed to the person of Moses, his birth and his death. On that subject he wrote what he himself called a "historical novel," a label which seems perfectly justified. He had strong hopes of having found a historic truth; he knew it was fiction but that it was well founded. The vacillation between the memory of reality and fantasy, which marked the first steps of his discovery, is found again in the last ones.

The arguments he used are plausible and invoke certain truths established by history, but they are not proof. He would have been on more solid ground if he had tried to analyze Moses' life as a myth. But what he was really looking for was an objective truth.

Here, probably, it is archaeology itself which should be invoked. As is well known, it fascinated him; he was eighteen years old when Troy was excavated. He envied Schliemann and imitated him in his own way. In this there was a wish displacement, quite apparent in the passion with which he collected archaeological objects. But there was something else: he had the impression that he had discovered the actual foundations of religion. Evidently there was nothing to that, since his Moses was only transmitting religion. What he found the origins of in history was guilt, as he had found them in prehistory at the time of *Totem and Taboo*.

He carried to the most extreme lengths some hypotheses advanced by specialists of a certain type of history —biblical history—which in itself invites speculation. However, it is an established fact that a monotheistic sect once existed in Egypt. The Pharaoh Ikhnaton made the god Aton the only god and suppressed all the other cults. In 1912, Abraham had published a study on that subject. Freud had forgotten it, but it is likely that his interest in Egyptian monotheism was sparked by Abraham's paper.

It was also agreed that Moses' name was Egyptian. But from that Freud deduced that Moses *was* Egyptian; he saw the proof of it in the myth of his birth, similar to so many other myths of the birth of heroes. (However, he adopted a hypothesis advanced by others: that there were two Moseses, one of whom was Jewish in spite of his name, which runs somewhat counter to his argument.) When he supposed that Moses had brought the monotheism of the Egyptians to the Jews, he did not borrow that idea from anyone; but when he had his Moses fall under the blows of a people in revolt (recapitulating an idea from *Totem and Taboo*), he had some few authors on his side (for instance, Ernst Sellin).

In a manner reminiscent of the end of *Totem and Taboo*, the guilt which followed Moses' murder was the foundation of a new social order. Naturally, it no longer was related to a general transformation of humanity but to the history of the Jewish and Christian peoples.

While he was writing this book in Vienna (he rewrote it several times), he was in mortal danger from the Nazis. But he accepted that danger with an indifference perhaps understandable at his age: "It is a death like any other," he said. That indifference was even more surprising because we know that he was full of anxiety—it may be called panic—at the thought that his book might provoke the Catholic authorities of Vienna and Rome.

He had pondered the risks he was running when, in 1927, he was about to publish *The Future of an Illusion*, in which he attacked religion. He had unemotionally gone ahead with it. But fifteen years before, he had been panic-stricken when he published the end of *Totem and Taboo*, where the father is murdered. That latter book, however, could only irritate anthropologists. It is certain that, for him, the murder of the father was the very knot of the feeling of guilt and, so to speak, the place where it could be untied. Hence, *Moses and Monotheism* is not to be taken as a simple historical novel; it sought distant verities which were like the last and most solemn echo of the Oedipus complex, discovered at the end of the last century. At the same time, the identification with the father made Freud see his own death in that of Moses.

What a journey, at once necessary and unpredictable it had been! From the paradoxes of posthypnotic amnesia, where it all began, through the pleasure principle, to end in the death drive, the murder of the father, and the ineradicable sense of guilt! Freud's identification with Moses was conscious and cultivated. Long before, he had identified with Christopher Columbus. He had written to Fliess: ". . . for I am not really a man of science, not an observer, not an experimenter, and not a thinker. I am nothing but by temperament a *conquistador* . . ."[98] Columbus had discovered a continent but had not given his name to it. Moses likewise had led his people to the promised land but had not entered it himself. Freud was always convinced that he would not personally profit from his discoveries.

But when he had to flee Austria and seek refuge in England—accompanied by his daughter Anna, whom he could not do without because of so many crippling operations—when the man the Viennese allowed to leave as a culprit saw himself welcomed in London as a hero, it is impossible that in the face of that ultimate and brief gift from fate, he did not once more think of Oedipus and of the sanctuary at Colonus. If not, then it was because that identification was by far the most meaningful.

The Future of a Disillusion

ALMOST FROM THE BEGINNING
Freud was concerned with what the future of psychoanalysis would be when it was no longer under his direct
influence—or after his death. In outlining what that future
was, two different approaches are available to me.

The first is historical, and is the one most commonly
employed. If this method is used we must describe the
various events marking the development and growth of
psychoanalysis, explaining how in certain countries the
authorities halted its growth, the resistances it had to
overcome elsewhere, and in what stages it gained acceptance in the different areas of public opinion.

The second approach is more difficult, and it may
never have been systematically followed. Quite often
analysts have described one particular aspect of psychoanalysis, but always in order to define more precisely
their own positions (perhaps there is no other way), and
we are still left without an overall view. In attempting to
achieve such a view we would ask in what way, in which
direction, and under what influences the corpus of the
doctrine Freud left us—both theory and technique—has
been modified in various countries. In certain cases these

modifications have resulted from the necessity of adapting
Freud's concepts to tasks he had not undertaken—for instance, the treatment of the early stages of schizophrenia.
In other situations one can discover the influence of ideologies alien to Freud's preoccupations and deriving from
medical modes of thinking, from the norms of the experimental sciences, from empirical philosophy, from the
postulates of behaviorism or evolutionism or general psychology, and even from the preconceptions of ethics or
sociology. The issue then would be to determine whether
those foreign influences have enlarged or enriched the
analytic doctrine, or whether they have been conducive
to a kind of regression which has risked burying or per-
verting it.

I do not have all the information required to employ
confidently this second approach, the only one that truly
interests me. What I am able to say about it may perhaps
encourage those who do have the information to attempt
it. Even my errors could lead to very desirable clarifica-
tions. And after all, I can comfort myself with the
thought (unfortunately debatable) that for a writer who
only wants to identify major trends an overly complete
documentation runs the danger of creating as many
difficulties and obscurities as advantages. Finally, I must
remember that I am necessarily situated in a certain perspective and that I can only describe things as they may
appear from Paris. I am sure I will remember this, because
I cannot do otherwise.

Freud always felt his discovery had no guarantee of
a future. From the start he had measured the violence
of the opposition it created, and the schisms which had
divided his "movement," as he himself called it, meant
only one thing to him: they were the result of a lack of
character, a cowardice in the face of prevalent opinion.
Among the dissidents he had identified that temptation

which leads to the most serious weakness: catering to the public's resistances and compromising with them.

The question is whether the lesson he thus taught us has become irrelevant, whether Freud's courage was only necessary in the beginning and if today it may not have become anachronistic. In any event, as far as he was concerned, he was convinced that it was in the very nature of the psychoanalytic doctrine to appear shocking and subversive. On board ship to America he did not feel he was bringing that country a new panacea. With his typically dry wit he told his traveling companions, "We are bringing them the plague."

Drawing on two personal examples, he saw a way of assuring the future of a doctrine which inspired such great hostility. Around 1852, before his birth, Emil Du Bois-Reymond, Ernst Brücke, and Hermann von Helmholtz had banded together to form a kind of scientific freemasonry, out of which would later emerge the "Physikalische Gesellschaft" of Berlin whose goal was to completely destroy whatever remained of the old vitalist ideology. This conspiracy—which Freud joined in spirit— had had the greatest possible success.

The other less well known example dated from the end of his secondary studies. Under the influence of a schoolmate at the Sperl Gymnasium, Heinrich Braun, he had long considered joining a clandestine political group of the opposition as an activist.

It is not quite clear if Jones knew or had guessed Freud's intention to imitate these models. As Jones himself explained it was shortly before World War I, in the early days of the International Society, that he proposed the creation of a "strictly secret" committee to guide the society's policies and to defend the scientific interests of psychoanalysis. This proposal fulfilled Freud's intentions.

There is a law—not restricted to societies of analysts

—that when a group is organized to defend a cause it does indeed assure and promote the growth of that cause, but at the same time it also creates the possibility of conflicts arising between the interests of the cause it is protecting and those of the organization itself. For example, the formation of communist parties helped spread Marxist doctrine; but it also considerably encumbered that doctrine with the task of defending the party's structure, and it is not easy to do as Mao did—attack his own party to preserve the purity of the doctrine. Once an analytic society was founded, there was no way for it to avoid these difficulties.

They appeared almost immediately, or in any case very early, if the war years are excluded from the chronology. Freud was then and always remained a champion of lay analysis. Jones was president of the Association; Freud kept him in that post not so much because of his ideological abilities (they were real, but Ferenczi or Abraham would have done at least as well), but because he wanted a foreign and non-Jewish president. In the matter of lay analysis Jones was in complete agreement with Freud, but he also had to think of the preservation of the Association. The American analysts, for reasons historically explicable (American physicians had only recently obtained legal protection against charlatans), were opposed to the principle of lay analysis and were ready to resign. Therefore, as president, Jones found himself obliged to stifle his convictions as an analyst and to attempt to sway Freud. One can imagine that it was not an easy task. We know the problem was amicably settled through a compromise: each national society would solve it the way it thought best.

This conflict was more important for its symptomatic value than in and of itself. It revealed the indirect effect that the organization—indispensable in one form or another of course—of the analytic profession could have on doctrinal positions, the very ones it might be called upon to defend.

I have said I did not intend to write a step-by-step history; furthermore, I could not do it in an area where access to all the information would impose on the writer an obligation to be discreet. But it can be seen how in all countries, France included, the mechanical workings of the organization may result in exposing complicated problems which are of some importance in the doctrine's conservation and propagation.

Every psychoanalytic society is required to establish its own rules for the recruitment and training of new members. (It is apparent we are not so far removed from the problem created by lay analysis for Freud and Jones.) It was entirely logical that a candidate be initially required to undergo analysis and that he thereafter accept the supervision of an experienced analyst. It was completely out of the question that analysis be taught by academic methods. More ancient and more venerable methods had to be revived, those which had governed the ancient systems of apprenticeship, of initiation into the silent school of Pythagoras—and which still govern certain Buddhist sects. All this was fully justified and fully in accord with the essence of psychoanalysis. Besides, it would function perfectly well for a long time.

As long a time, it seems, as analysis was not an accepted fact, as it was disputed, as it had not become completely respectable. In that already distant period it was almost entirely neurotics who entered analysis seeking to escape their torments. They would come prepared to accept the patient's role, to identify with it and to discover, as Freud had with Fliess, the indispensable element of analysis in the suffering of transference—after which it was relatively easy to add on all its teachable aspects. It often happened—it still often happens—that a patient in analysis would discover within himself an analyst's "vocation"; that wish could be analyzed and could sometimes be realized. Not all the early recruits of analysis took that road; sometimes the chronological order was reversed, and an "original" proposed himself as a candidate right off. But in that instance the analyst would certainly treat the candidacy as just one symptom among others, as a defense against analysis itself, and everything would be restored to analytical order. I omit mentioning here the way in which Freud himself accepted his first disciples. That story would require a very judicious historical analysis.

In establishing rules for the training of analysts the only intention was to recognize the technical necessity of a preliminary analysis. But the very fact that a set of rules existed would totally alter the situation. The preliminary analysis inevitably became the trial—the initiation rite—which opened the way to a career. Candidates who did not feel the need of subjecting themselves to analysis bowed to that rule because it had become obligatory. And since they were generally medical students, psychiatric interns, or psychologists, it would seem that their professional training and their apparent normality were good signs. I cannot enumerate all the many other factors involved: the analysts' desire to be promoted to the level of teacher; the fact that it was not very pleasant, in the course of a treatment, to have to discourage the vocational "calling" that occurred unexpectedly in a patient who had no aptitude for it. All this made it more convenient that requirements be determined at the start, and that it be understood beforehand whether an analysis was a training analysis or a therapy.

A new kind of analysand was created. These candidates naturally identified with their analysts and not with the patient, and they found themselves in the classic psychiatric segregation (the others are the ones who are sick; I am the doctor). Analysis probably possessed the means of dislodging them from that false role—but taking that stand ran the risk of doing away with analysis. It was sometimes difficult to reject someone after he had been accepted as a candidate, after he had obeyed all the rules, without any result but meekly and zealously, for several years. Moreover, owing to a questionable theoretical attitude, an analyst might find some satisfaction in being the object of identification of one who was no longer his patient but his pupil.

The consequences of this new state of affairs did not appear to be catastrophic (not enough so, I feel). The candidate did not become a real analyst but he nevertheless possessed the psychotherapeutic methods available to nonanalysts, and furthermore he benefitted from a knowledge of Freudian doctrine and from certain very useful rules of technique. In this way he achieved results sufficient to satisfy him and to encourage him in continuing to develop by acquiring experience. After all, Freud had undergone his analysis with Fliess; a fairly gifted patient can make an analysis with a pseudoanalyst, but it must be admitted that such gifted patients are quite rare. One may speculate pleasantly on the attitude Freud would have taken in the earliest days if he had had to appear as a candidate before some of the societies we know today.

I am not maliciously attacking a hidden flaw in the training of analysts. I am only remarking on a marked malaise which preoccupies analysts in every country, as can be seen in their specialized publications. The Inter-

national Association, in the spirit of Freud's great toler-
ance (he knew, however, when to draw the line), has not
needed to any large extent to combat doctrinal heresies.
But it was confronted by real difficulties in the matter
of recruitment. At a recent Congress in Rome one could
observe some defiant symbolic (and symptomatic) ges-
tures by young and not-so-young European analysts.

But it had not been necessary to wait that long to
observe the symptoms. In France, where I am reasonably
knowledgeable about the situation, we have witnessed
three splits since the end of World War II. They were
all caused by this problem. The first occurred because a
training program for analysts was not unanimously
adopted. The second resulted from the question of
whether or not to accept international regulations. The
third came about because a group of analysts—actually
quite small—could not agree to an organizational project
on admission procedures for new colleagues. Naturally,
as always, there were other reasons below the surface, but
they have always crystallized around this kind of problem. Even today, the matter is still on the agenda in
France. In various ways, according to the different societies, there is a tendency to revise practices which until
now have been accepted. For example, one is suspicious
of candidates who are simply out to make a career.
Medical training is no longer considered a sufficient indication. One goes so far as to demand a certain amount
of neurosis from the candidate (one wonders about the
consequences of that requirement, if it risks encouraging
a quasi-simulation). As yet there have been only attempts
and halfhearted efforts to find a solution, and it is not
clear one will be found, since psychoanalysis has ceased
to be a "plague" and in fact become a career. A perusal
of foreign publications enables us to see that the same

problem is encountered elsewhere. Haven't we heard ambitious but honorable analysts confess, after a completely successful training analysis, that they had almost secretly undertaken another analysis in order to "cure" their neuroses?

These characteristics are symptomatic of a crisis, which itself results from farsighted, prudent, and wise measures—and perhaps also from a too-long delayed official recognition that they had become inadequate. It is therefore quite reassuring to see that there are young analysts less preoccupied with their careers than with the intention of defending something psychoanalysis is in danger of losing. This also is part of fidelity to Freud.

The question already posed by Freud about the future of psychoanalysis can be considered from another standpoint. It may be inseparable from the first, for if the recruitment of analysts is compromised over the issue of their training the transmission and refinement of the doctrine they bear will also be fatally compromised. Freud did not anticipate that the societies whose creation he favored would perform only a custodian's role, nor that they would only achieve a greater expansion of analytical practice through cautious recruitment. He considered his work open both to corrections and to new developments. Having science as a model, it was not liable to either limitation or completion. It is true that in this field research does not depend on organizations or on any regulations—or if so, only in a very indirect way. If we evaluate the research being done along lines parallel and contemporaneous to Freud's own, as well as after him, we will discover a few rewards in it, but certainly less important ones than he might have hoped for. Only as a matter of convenience, let us quickly touch on the state of research in several countries.

In England romantic writing often took the form of biography, the hero's destiny being determined by his childhood and his education. It is in the area of these literary and moral traditions and not in that of theory (empiricism and Darwinism, for example) that we must seek an explanation for the fact that psychoanalysis has been able to acclimatize itself a little more quickly in England than elsewhere. Perhaps also an already shaky vestige of Victorian prejudices awaited one decisive push which would remove it. From abroad, Melanie Klein brought an inspired idea—deriving from Ferenczi and above all from Abraham—which enabled her to discover the theoretical and procedural means to ultimately create a true psychoanalysis out of the half-educational children's therapy, something Anna Freud herself had not yet dared do. The value of what was new in the Kleinian concepts was quickly verified by the use one could make of them in the treatment of psychotic adults; it was a major advance at the time. Michael Balint—also under the distant influence of Ferenczi—was later to move away from the impenetrable mysteries of psychosomatic illness and, as we have seen, to clinically discover a solution to the problem of medicine's relationship to psychoanalysis. The Englishman D. W. Winnicott, pursuing a different but parallel course, had already discovered in the impasses of pediatrics the necessity of having recourse to analysis.

For a while, England, the heir to Freud's remains—as Athens was to those of Oedipus—found itself the leader of the European analytic movement.

It is a difficult and dangerous task to delineate only the major outlines of the point to which the English school has brought analytic theory. To begin with, I believe we should indicate the difference, minute at the time, which separated Abraham and Freud. As we know, Freud confined himself to the identification with the object, while Abraham stressed the incorporation of the object; and while Freud tried to go back as far as infantile neurosis, Abraham saw in the initial incorporation stages which already possessed psychotic characteristics. It is this orientation which Melanie Klein brought from Berlin to England in positing the hypothesis of a conflict between the self of the subject and the incorporated objects —universalizing, so to speak, hypochondria, melancholia, mania, and paranoia, as they were understood according to Abraham. In place of the identification conflict, located within the framework of a self conceived of as *imaginary*, was the opposition of a self (which should be called "real") to the interior object.

This point of departure—which was somewhat fruitful—resulted in what is called the object relation in its various aspects becoming the center of concern. The pleasure principle which dominated Freudian metapsychology (where it is almost identical with the primary process, which it is evidently impossible to give up without renouncing the unconscious itself, and without which there is no longer any kind of psychoanalysis possible) was re-examined in the light of an object relation *situated in reality*, in a kind of biological context. In that context, to be sure, the pleasure principle took on the aspect of hedonistic or utilitarian philosophy, and it was very easy to rely on pure and simple observation (and not on analysis) to prove that the human subject was not determined by the irresistible attraction of agreeable sensations, at least much less so than by his attachment or hostility to objects. So far this approach contained nothing to contradict Freud, who had not hesitated to say, for example, that separation from the object was the cause of displeasure. He could only be contradicted in a biological context, for in the latter is found neither organ nor sensation to explain the displeasure of separation. In Freud's theory the subject obeys the pleasure principle when separation is disastrous for him and the reality principle when he has learned to control it; that control operates through symbolization, as is shown by the following example from *Beyond the Pleasure Principle*. Freud had caught a young child just in the process of learning that symbolic control through the reiterated words "o-o-o-o" and "da." For Freud it was not the presence of the object, however gratifying, that could provide a satisfactory solution (this would imply dependence on the pleasure principle), because that would lead to stagnation and retardation. It was the absence of the object, the only source of symbolic thought, that was the introduction to the reality principle—for that principle never implied that possession of the object was more real than its absence (which would mean adopting the pleasure principle!) but that the *reality to be controlled* was precisely the absence of the object! A reading of Freud (instead of imputing to him the very naïve and commonplace ideas he was trying to rid us of) is enough to overcome these nonexistent difficulties. The absence of the object is the very condition necessary for the developmnt of symbolic thought, and even though Freud did not in those words add it to his study on negation, where it rightly belonged, one nevertheless finds its scattered elements throughout his entire works.

We might imagine that Winnicott had gone even further with biologically oriented interpretations because of his stress on the *real* frustrations the object can inflict on the subject (the child). But actually he did not get lost in that dead end. A sure clinical sense and faultless experimentation always corrected the errors into which his theoretical principles might have led him. For example, he is the inventor of the concept of the *transitional object*, which is obviously the exact though silent equivalent of the *da* of the child Freud observed. If Winnicott failed to explain that equivalency, what he has written on this subject presupposes it. The transitional object is already part of a symbolism and almost of a language, a fact which escapes those who confound *language* and *communication*.

It is therefore not entirely impossible (not yet) to interpret the English theoretical postures in the light of pure Freudian metapsychology. But it is doubtful that the English are at present convinced of the necessity of trying to clarify matters along this line. Therefore, they run the risk—if they get so far away from the symbolic area and from language as to lose sight of them completely, and if they unremittingly commit themselves to a biological approach—of cutting British psychoanalysis off from its only sources of inspiration and of rendering it sterile. Biologically speaking, what could be more satisfying than pairing off the subject and the gratifying object (and who is not aware that the Oedipus complex is biologically meaningless?), but to put such a theory into practice would be just the same as giving up culture (I mean the cultural minimum possessed by even the Australian aborigines)! And in daily clinical practice we clearly see how some form of fusion of the subject with the gratifying object is at the root of debilitated states.

In France, psychoanalysis was long present as a foreign body. Through the efforts of Joseph Babinski, medical positivism had completely repudiated Charcot's observations on hysterics, and the fact that psychoanalysis had used them as a starting point cast a pall of suspicion over it. Psychology in France was above all academic; its pedagogic applications (entirely empirical) were limited to measurements. Nor did sociology seek any broad application. Medicine and psychiatry were almost completely impenetrable and the distrust of the religious was expressed in scorn and silence. A few specialists (such as Charles Blondel), judging the truth of psychoanalysis according to the kind of experience they had had, rejected it in good faith, without realizing that analysis was just another type of experience. The surrealistic literary circles showed the greatest interest in it, but that was basically because they sought to run away from it by using it as a poetic art. With good reason, Freud considered France the most resistant country.

However, psychoanalysis finally showed some signs of growth in France; it had fervent missionaries, like Marie Bonaparte, but they were not making any original contributions. One had the impression that in this period books on psychoanalysis, and not only those in French, repeated and copied each other just as did pietistic books in the preceding centuries.

After World War II, attention began to be paid to the work of theoretical revision begun by Jacques Lacan. He had undertaken to systematize what Freud's texts had given us, and to distinguish what was original and irreducible at the source of his discovery. Intransigent in regard to theoretical orientation and in sharp opposition to the Establishment, Lacan gradually came to deeply influence analytic thought, even that of his avowed adversaries. It is to him that we owe the very faithful and very creative rebirth of Freudianism in France. Until now, only one book has appeared in English which enables one to have some idea of Lacan's point of view: *The Language of the Self* by Anthony Wilden, published in 1968 by the John Hopkins Press in Baltimore. Lacan's influence has extended beyond the profession into intellectual circles, where psychoanalysis was on the point of being condemned or ignored because of the inconsistency and theoretical sterility from which it had not emerged.

The present work, in which it is not possible to do justice to Lacan's theory (that would take another book), derives its inspiration from his general orientation.

A discussion of the brilliant start the "movement" had in Berlin and of the ways in which it was stopped by the authorities is better left to historians. However, it is interesting to note that while Melanie Klein's influence in England tended to be limited to analytic schools which, in a manner of speaking, monopolized it, in countries where it was allowed to develop freely it had a seminal effect on research. For example, in Argentina, from which have come incontestably new contributions.

However, it is in the United States that the practice of psychoanalysis has seen its greatest growth. Not only is the number of practitioners of analysis greater than in any other country, but the influence of Freudian ideas, at the expense of some distortions, has extended beyond the psychoanalytic world to social work, counseling, psychotherapy, etc. Psychoanalysts as such are much more numerous relative to the population than in any European country—and probably more numerous in absolute figures than the total of their European colleagues. This sheer statistical weight gives Americans a dominant influence over the world's psychoanalysts. From this point of view the United States has become the country where psychoanalysis has enjoyed its greatest success; it is there that the center of gravity of world psychoanalysis is located. What may be surprising, therefore, is that Europeans experience a certain distaste in seeking their inspiration from America. They behave as if that area of highest psychoanalytic density were a void as far as theoretical developments are concerned. I obviously cannot go beyond the ascertainment of that fact, nor can I decide whether the Europeans are right or wrong. It is not even clear that their attitude is consistently the result of the same motivation. The only thing I can do is try to state exactly how a European is able to adopt an attitude which obviously calls for an explanation. I must refrain from inquiring whether this attitude is fair or unfair. It is possible that it is due to a simple misunderstanding, and in that case my probing of the issue ought to settle the question. Somehow, something must be done about the paradoxical relations we have with American psychoanalysis. If it is just a matter of not really understanding it, in spite of the material in publications, then communications will have to be improved.

The disciples who brought the new doctrine to America were of the same kind as those who introduced it into England. However, things turned out differently.* It was immediately accepted as an evident fact—which it was not—that in order to become Americanized analysis had to be domesticated; in European countries, on the other hand, the people interested in it had only to "adapt" themselves to it.

The idea of adaptation—or of adjustment—did not have the same meaning in Darwin's fatherland as it had in the United States. In the latter, it had lost its purely

---

* I will not take into consideration here the doctrinal distortions encountered in several countries (for example, under the influence of medical ideology).

scientific character because the United States, throughout its history, had had to deal with problems of acculturation. The "adaptation" of the individual (an immigrant) to "reality"—geographical or social—had a meaning the word did not have elsewhere.

Even as late as 1949, the American psychologist Ernest Hilgard declared before a meeting of the American Psychological Association that the mechanisms of adjustment were the features of Freudian theory that were domesticated earliest into American psychology. This is an astonishing statement, if one remembers that the theory constructed by Freud (in this context it is perhaps necessary to distinguish it from "Freudian theory") did not in the slightest degree make adjustment either a basic issue or a therapeutic goal. (No such word even appears in the indexes of Freud's works.) In Europe we feel that Hilgard would have been more accurate if he had said, "The concept of adjustment was the first that American psychology injected into the Freudian theory in order to *domesticate it*."

In brief, psychoanalysis was expected to consider itself an immigrant.

This point of departure, which may not have been adequately taken into account in analysis or the history of ideologies, has—according to us, naturally—decisively stamped the development of analytic theory. On the other hand, the development of practice increased the demand and made analysis, more than in other countries, a social and moral *obligation* and gave the unconscious remnant of puritanical tendencies a safety valve perhaps completely necessary to provide a transition, in order that the revolution brought about by analysis might be accepted.

The "modernist" illusion—namely that the changes

occurring in the environment force a readaptation of the very principles of psychoanalysis as Freud posited them —itself obviously depends on prejudices tied to the notion of adjustment. Freud never concerned himself with the adaptation of his patients to the society of his time; he enabled them to solve their problems themselves, and their relationship to their milieu was one of them—no more and no less, for example, than their marital relationship, one he did not treat at all on a realistic plane as a counselor would have.

In the transformation of society Freud would certainly have seen a source of repression in no way different from the old forms of repression, except insofar as the fact that success in this world tends to be substituted for success in the other—that is to say, in morality—which may simplify problems but does not make them any easier. And Freud would certainly have credited to the return of repressed material those crimes and mental illnesses which ordinary people directly attribute to the pressures of modern life on the individual. For the effect of that pressure is indirect and cannot be understood outside the hypothesis that it is actually the very pressure of repression. Modern life has not changed anything in the structure of the ego. It has increased the weight of the repressed material which threatens it, and the preponderance given the ego could ultimately serve the (non-Freudian) ideal of "achieving a successful repression," as if that were the only means of "adapting" to reality. In any case, it is a difficult question which must be considered very seriously.

From the purely scientific viewpoint, there is a disparity, a real split, between the more or less explicit utilization by theoreticians of empiricist premises they accept (such as those of Darwinism and of behaviorism) and the epistemology of present-day science (one forfeits this evidence if one confuses the development of science with the success of technology, which can rightly be interpreted in terms of biological adaptation). It appears that the linguists, who had for so long and even sometimes unwittingly agreed to the empirical-behaviorist viewpoint, appreciated the change more quickly than psychoanalysts. Noam Chomsky's work, for instance, postulates that language is not a form of behavior. His position would not startle the analysts. All he did was to rejoin Freud whose theories on these questions were far ahead of the postulates of his era's human sciences—and in his time the specialists of those sciences had naturally criticized him. It was of course impossible to construct a theory to justify psychoanalytic technique without adopting a specific position on the nature of language, be that position either explicit or implicit. Obviously, it was preferable that it be explicit.

To stress adjustment is to treat the patient as a kind of immigrant undergoing *acculturation*—by stating it this way one can see the anachronistic nature of that concept; it is explained as a trait of the individual or collective past and already constitutes a kind of survival in the present world. For it must be recognized that an immigrant quite talented in criminal activities adapts (in the scientific and Darwinian sense) more quickly to the society he enters than the one who reveals a docile honesty. And then, it is society which, always in the Darwinian sense of the word, has to adapt to that kind of immigrant —that is to say, to develop defenses which will necessarily not be completely adequate. Thinking about these questions clearly demonstrates to one that the prevalent (and nonscientific) use made of the concept of adaptation conceals hidden postulates which are on the level of the most rudimentary social morality: Everybody has to be like everybody else.

This old postulate of social conformism is only slightly different from the way in which the feeling of identity appears in the modern world. The evolution of that feeling ultimately tends to shake the belief each person has in his *uniqueness* and not in his *identity*. That feeling of uniqueness has its origin in the initial family relationships—in a family each member is irreplaceable, recognized, and loved simply *because he is*. The identifications which are mingled in it will not alter anything, and in a latent form the feeling of uniqueness exists prior to that of identity. When the child starts school, perspectives change, the child becomes replaceable, and he is recognized for what he does; later on, this will be stressed even more. This is the way it has always been—at least since the decline of the aristocratic ideal. Modern life has simply reinforced this phenomenon. Today's notion that everyone should come off an assembly line exactly alike in order for the social machine to function effectively is no more than a transformation of the old imperative: Everybody must be like everybody else so that we may all recognize each other as nice people.

To a psychoanalyst that is a very superficial transformation. The feeling of uniqueness, spontaneous in childhood, is always present and has only been repressed. It is quite easy to see how that repressed material can return, for example, in individual "exploits" which can either be socially acceptable or completely antisocial. If, as Erik Erikson states so precisely, identity must be achieved (and he is clinically correct), it is simply because uniqueness must be repressed. Identity is nothing but the socially accepted form of lost uniqueness. And psychoanalysts are in a good position to perceive as much in transference manifestations as in erotic states, a demand for uniqueness on the part of the neurotic patient.

If adjustment remains, overtly or not, the essential preoccupation that casts its shadow over the theoretical thought of American psychoanalysis, we believe we understand the direction that theory has taken. Of course, there was no doubt that the vehicle of adjustment had to be the ego. Actually, the idea that such a psychical necessity is required in order to treat this kind of problem is not Freudian—Freud only used it—since it goes back to antiquity, where Plato had already attributed this function to "the governing part of the soul." (And Saint Paul showed how it could be in a state of conflict over the government of the self.)

What is truly Freudian is the discovery that the ego is the object of narcissism, that it belongs to the imaginary order, that it can in some way be "other" than ourselves, an image in which we can alienate ourselves—particularly in psychosis.

Before there had been any question of stressing the ego, Karen Horney, a psychoanalyst probably already influenced by her adjustment to American thought, had admitted that the therapeutic goal was the adaptation of the patient to the environment. Her theory, which is close enough to Freud's in its principles, strikes us by its sense of rightness and great intelligence. But we immediately notice that with the orientation she gave it there is absolutely no possibility of using it in a fairly serious case of hysteria or obsessional neurosis. (She would not have been able to treat either the "Rat Man" or the "Wolf Man" without extending her technique, to say nothing of a case of incipient schizophrenia.)

On the other hand, once it is accepted that the goal of therapy is adaptation to social conditions, it is inevitable that some theory of the social order, such as a cultural anthropology, be joined to psychoanalysis; this is the point, in our opinion, where *culturalism* enters into American psychoanalysis. Evidently, one could not argue —as a gravedigger nearly does in Hamlet—that what is neurotic in one culture would be normal in another; that it is sufficient to send a Dane to England to cure him of his madness, which is no more than an imperfect adaptation to Danish culture. Of course, the positions taken by culturalists are not so naïve, but the fact is that they cannot convince us they were not born out of a problem peculiar to America, and that they were not the deferred effect of that old problem.

In any case, so far as Karen Horney is concerned, it is apparent that some culturalism was mandatory in her system, but that is because she was not too demanding when it came to matters on a pathologic level. Patients troubled by cultural or environmental change—who of course exist—can benefit from her treatment, but such cases are far from encompassing the entire field of psychopathology.

The formulations of the partisans of ego psychology —Heinz Hartmann, Rudolph Lowenstein, Ernst Kris, *et al.*—in one sense go much further along the path Horney pioneered. She had only been interested in the adaptation to others, to social or interpersonal relationships. In ego psychology it cannot be said that the problem of adaptation to reality is presented—its definition remains superficial—but that adaptation to reality is made the aim of psychic development and the criterion of mental health. It is not easy to give a short summary of the theoretical positions of the ego psychologists and do them full justice, for their works contain a number of statements from which psychoanalysis can greatly profit. And in

summing up their fundamental beliefs, which appear
fragile to us, their works are necessarily presented in the
most unfavorable light. Hartmann's theory, for instance,
claims in principle that the ego does not derive from the
id but from a nondifferentiated point of origin, out of
which both ego and id proceed simultaneously. However,
the ego brings with it a heredity—which could be called
Darwinian—that means it is already in a sense adapted to
the "probable" reality; it comes, as it were, into the world
prepared for whatever it may encounter there. This concept's biological inspiration is obvious. This first adaptation, which would suppose a primary autonomy of the
ego in relation to drives, must make way for a secondary
autonomy which will allow adaptation to the actual situation in which the patient finds himself. This secondary
autonomy provides something which in a language other
than Hartmann's would be called a position of "objectivity."

It is important to note that Hartmann was the first
to realize fully that this kind of objectivity was not nearly
sufficient. First, it would be necessary somehow to make
a place and leave a role for what we, in contradistinction,
call subjectivity. Furthermore, Hartmann himself had a
clear idea of the importance of the retreat movement, by
which the patient turns away from actual reality to
elaborate a symbolism (language, then mathematics)
which alone will permit him to master it. But he does
not see that from that moment on he can no longer preserve the hypothetical bases which served him at the start.

Taken on a too elementary level, the theory of adaptation leads to contradictions which the authors do not
hide from us.

Hartmann writes that "the nature of the environment may be such that a pathological development of

the psyche offers a more satisfactory solution than would a normal one."[99] From this it follows that neurosis is a form of adaptation. But in that event, if we recognize the pathological character of that adaptation, by what criterion do we recognize it? By invoking another environment? For if we pretend to dispense with a criterion that is not a form of adaptation to an environment, we would abandon the hypotheses of ego psychology, and it is easy to show that the notion of adaptability (in contradistinction to adaptation) does not provide a solution, since the environment to which we must adapt may be such that a pathological development of the psyche would offer a more satisfactory solution. This is true unless adaptability is correctly defined: namely, as the ability to *disadapt* oneself. For man has always been adapted, in the Darwinian sense of the word. He constantly disadapts himself by modifying the environment. Besides, for Darwin there is only one criterion for adaptation: the simple fact of remaining alive.

Naturally, a school that has become so important cannot be discussed in a few lines. But there is neither ego psychoanalysis, nor id psychoanalysis, nor superego psychoanalysis. There is, as Hartmann clearly states, an ego psychology which can be psychoanalytic. It would not be difficult to show the influence of biology (adaptation to the environment), of psychology (the individual is a synthesis), of morality and of religion (the creature must have a principle of autonomy capable of assuming responsibility for his faults but also of overcoming his natural temptations).

In 1930, Freud himself had severely criticized the tendency to amalgamate into psychoanalysis the viewpoints of other human sciences, for example, other psychological schools. He had written (using English terms) that he did not see that tendency as a proof of "broad-mindedness" but rather of a "lack of judgment."[100]

We believe that Erik Erikson is an analyst of great stature, and we admire his case histories and his biographies, wherein he demonstrates a flawless clinical sense. In the case history of Sam (to select one example among the many), in the first pages of his *Childhood and Society*, we can clearly see the role played by the unsaid, by the denial of the right to know, by the effects of the repressed material's return depending on the circumstances, and by transference and the effects of interpretation. All this is presented to us in a brilliant fashion. Everything depends on what is *said* and what is *not* said. Even the symbolism of games—which has its place in this case history—functions like a language. The *fort* and *da* Freud observed could relevantly be mentioned in it. But the theoretical construction that Erikson erects on it disturbs us; it implies that nothing which happened to Sam would have happened had he not belonged to a Jewish family in the process of adjusting to a non-Jewish environment —and we cannot agree with this because we know almost identical cases where no cultural problem was involved. We see how the problem of adjustment was inserted into that splendid case history. We can see elsewhere— and Erikson says so himself—that his theory of identity is rather closely tied to that of the ego and forms a kind of appendage to it.

I am well aware that so few examples so summarily analyzed cannot cover the enormous and impressive extent of American work. And there has been no attempt to make them do so. I have used them to express myself, to try to sustain a possible thesis—one which I believe is worth discussing—that as soon as Freudian analysis reached America, it was immediately absorbed into a pseudo-

Darwinian ideology of social adjustment. I am of course not able to state whether or not Freudian psychoanalysis has gained or lost by this. I can simply offer the truism that psychoanalysis has become something different from what it is in Europe and that the two branches have difficulty in establishing a dialogue. Furthermore, I have an idea that in this area I have been referring to the recent past rather than to the present.

Nevertheless, the greatest danger psychoanalysis faces does not come from the innovations and distortions Freud's successors might contribute to it. It is already hardened against that threat, and while Freud was alive it triumphed over all deviations.

There are many examples in history to teach us that a truly new thought must first meet the test or the threat of being buried by the previous way of thinking, by traditional thought. Galileo's physics, which broke with all the accepted ideas of the scholars of his day, soon suffered a setback and was watered down in Descartes's work; but what was original in Descartes was even further reduced by the Cartesians who followed him, and it was not until Newton appeared that the point of Galilean thought was rediscovered and pulled out from the quagmire of the metaphysical tradition. No one should be surprised if Freud's discovery encounters the same obstacles—even if metaphysics is no longer involved.

In the very beginning, psychoanalysis was, in Freud's own words "no more than a new medical procedure for influencing certain mental diseases," and this limited—therapeutic—field of application of the early years would always remain the only area in which psychoanalysis could verify its propositions and perfect itself. But it was by no means confined to that field, and there is some danger in keeping it within the medical framework it seemingly had in the beginning. One cannot, except in metaphor, speak of mental health the way one speaks of bodily health. It is not a factual matter, it is not our natural state as is the latter, and one cannot conceive of the analyst's function as being the restoration to mental health of those who through some accident have been deprived of it. At the same time what meaning can be given to an expression like "mental hygiene" when we know that in this area any attempt at inquiry, even a simple statistical survey, is already pathogenic? Real progress is not represented by the increase of medical knowledge alone; it is rather to be seen in the transformation of the attitude people who call themselves "normal" hold towards those they believe to be "sick." The label "sick," so useful when applied to someone physically incapable of fulfilling his obligations, can have, as is well known, a very different effect upon someone mentally troubled. Is such a sign not enough to demonstrate that it is not a question of two divisions of a single medicine, but of two disciplines of which only one is medical? Following Freud's example, psychoanalysts avoid applying the classification "sick" to their analysands or even making diagnoses or prognoses. To reduce the analyst to the role of physician and the neurotic to that of patient—although Freud in the early days used such language—would be to enroll the analysts in the ranks of the repressive powers.

It is sufficient to have observed how an analysis is inseparable from transference, how it unfolds by moving from reversals to recognitions—just as in the kind of tragedy Aristotle describes—to be convinced that what it reveals profoundly is a kind of original fracture in the way man is constituted, a split that opposes him to himself (and not to reality or to society) and exposes him to the attacks of his unconscious. This situation is equally true for those enclosed within the protective barriers of "sanity" and for those who have attempted to free themselves through the vagaries of "madness."

Clearly, it is not a question of venerating and piously preserving Freud's heritage: that would consign it to sterility. It is much wiser to consider that heritage the very imperfect beginnings of a "science" which remains to be elaborated upon in as open-ended a way as are the other sciences. But we must not forget that in this area resistances are always at work. They are quite prepared to accept psychoanalysis on condition that it be adapted in such a way that its most original contributions remain concealed. It is the originality of psychoanalysis that must be preserved and even rediscovered. It would be much less dangerous for Freud's work to be criticized and attacked by his opponents on the very points where it is most original than for it to be defended and championed by those who nibble away at its originality.

CHRONOLOGY

1856   May 6: Birth of Sigismund Freud (he will change his first name to Sigmund at twenty-two). According to tradition, he is also given a Jewish first name: Schlomo. His birthplace, Freiberg, Moravia, is now called Příbor. His father, Jakob Freud, a wool merchant, forty-one years old; had two children by a first marriage, Emmanuel and Philipp. Philipp had a son John, a year older than Sigismund (his uncle) and a little later to become his favorite playmate. Sigismund's mother twenty-one years old; Sigismund her first child. One unconfirmed family legend had the Freuds originating in Cologne.

         (In 1856, William James was ten years old, Nietzsche twelve, Hermann von Helmholtz thirty-five, Charcot thirty-one, Franz Brentano eighteen, Josef Breuer fourteen, G. T. Fechner fifty-five, Schopenhauer sixty-eight, and Johann Friedrich Herbart had died fifteen years before.)

1859   An economic crisis ruins Jakob Freud's business. The family settles down in straitened circumstances in Vienna (1860).

1865   Sigmund enters the Sperl Gymnasium a year ahead of time.

1870   He receives Ludwig Börne's complete works; they will have a great influence on him.

1872   A photograph shows us Freud at the awkward age: well-groomed, serious, a little pudgy, with the beginnings of a mustache; he does not at all resemble his later portraits. Returns to Freiberg to spend his vacation.

1873   Passes his final secondary-school exams *summa cum laude*. Congratulated on his literary style. Has already read a great deal in several languages. Influenced by a classmate (Heinrich Braun), he considers studying law. Decides on medicine after hearing a reading of the essay "On Nature," attributed to Goethe.

1874   At the University, he discovers anti-Semitic prejudices and feels that his place is with the "opposition." Takes Brentano's courses.

1875   Trip to England, to Manchester, and the home of his half-brother Philipp and his half-niece Pauline.

1876   First personal research on the gonadic structure of eels. Enters Ernst Brücke's laboratory.

1877   Publication of result of anatomical research on central nervous system of lamprey larva.

1878   In his research in Brücke's laboratory, comes close to discovery of the neuron (named in 1891 by Waldeyer). Forms a friendship with Josef Breuer, his elder by fourteen years, who helps him morally and materially (many loans of money).

1879   Unenthusiastically attends Meynert's psychiatry classes. Interested only in neurological aspect of problems.

1880   One year of military service. Breuer undertakes treatment of Bertha Pappenheim (Anna O.). Freud translates four essays by John Stuart Mill ("On the Question of Labour," "The Emancipation of Women," "Socialism," "Plato"). Wants to avoid practicing medicine and envisages a career in research or education.

1881   Takes (belatedly) final medical exams.

1882   Has to follow the advice of friends and professors: without material resources he could not pursue a researcher's career. He would have had to wait too long for a chair. He has met Martha Bernays (from an intellectual Jewish family) and wants to marry her: he has to earn a living. In November, Breuer speaks to him of Anna O.'s case, interrupted since June. Freud surprised, interested, but not influenced.

1883   Bored with general medicine; all he knows well is neurology. Enters Meynert's department of psychiatry. Has a glimpse of the role of desire in Meynert's amentia, but that accidental remark does not relate to his preoccupations.

1884   Asked to make a study of cocaine, he discovers its analgesic properties; suspects its anesthetic qualities but neglects them. Carl Koller will study them very successfully; that will not alter their good relationship. Freud imprudently uses cocaine himself. Not being disposed to toxicomania, he does not suffer from it and does not suspect its danger, but he causes others around him to be hurt. Wanting to cure his friend Fleischl, who is a morphine addict, he makes him a cocaine addict and aggravates his case. Is criticized in medical circles. Undertakes to treat "nervous" illnesses with electrotherapy, applying W. Erb's method. During the same period he perfects the coloring of neurological sections and publishes a paper on that subject, then a monograph on cocaine. Wants to gain recognition through some discovery.

1885   Occupies (for a short time) a post in a private hospital where hypnotism is occasionally used. In April, he destroys all his papers. For a while he thinks of emigrating to better his situation. Is named *Privatdozent*, then obtains a traveling scholarship and chooses to go to Paris, to Jean Charcot at the Salpêtrière. There he observes the manifestations of hysteria and the effects of hypnotism and suggestion. Charcot makes a great impression on him. He proposes himself as the German translator of Charcot's lectures and is accepted.

1886   Leaves Paris for Berlin, where he becomes interested in infantile neuropathology. Returning to Vienna, stays a while at the Institute for Children's Diseases. Gives a lecture on hysteria reporting on what he has observed with Charcot: it is badly received. Begins his private practice: opens his office on Easter Sunday. Marries Martha in September. Publishes translation of Charcot's *New Lectures on the Diseases of the Nervous System, Especially on Hysteria.*

1887   Without abandoning electrotherapy, begins to use hypnotism. Birth of Mathilde (October). First letter to Fliess (December).

1888   Publishes translation of Bernheim's book *On Suggestion and its Therapeutic Applications*. Applies for the first time a method inspired by Breuer (to Frau Emmy von N., in May).

1889   Trip to Nancy, to see H. M. Bernheim and A. A. Liébeault. Birth of Jean-Martin, named after Charcot (December).

1891   Publishes a book on aphasia, in which he criticizes the theory of localizations. Birth of Oliver (after Cromwell).

1892   Paper on hypnotic treatment. Succeeds in getting Breuer to collaborate with him. A patient (Elisabeth von R.) imposes the free-association method on him. Translation of Bernheim's second volume published. Birth of Ernst, named after Brücke.

1893   Publication of "Preliminary Communication" with Breuer. Writes Charcot's obituary (he had died August 16). Paper on hysterical paralysis (in French, in *Revue de Neurologie*). Formulation of the theory of traumatic seduction (which would have to be abandoned four years later). Birth of Sophia.

1894   Paper on "The Neuro-Psychoses of Defence." New Charcot translation (Clinical Lectures).

1895   Publication of "Obsessions and Phobias" and *Studies on Hysteria*. In July, at the Bellevue Châlet, near Vienna, analysis of the dream "Irma's Injection." Birth of Anna (December).

1896   Outbreak of violent negative feelings against Breuer. Scandalizes his audience with lecture on the sexual etiology of hysteria. Vacation in Florence. Death of Jakob Freud (October).

1897   Significant dream (oedipal, but explained by Freud through the trauma theory). Trip to Italy; does not go beyond Perusa (his identification with Hannibal makes him stop at Lake Trasimeno). Discovery of the Oedipus complex (October).

1898   Works on *The Psychopathology of Everyday Life* and assembles examples which will be used in *Jokes and Their Relation to the Unconscious*. Publishes "The

Psychical Mechanism of Forgetfulness." Completes *The Interpretation of Dreams* (except for Chapter 7).

1899   In Dresden, Joseph Popper-Lynkeus publishes *Phantasies of a Realist*, which Freud will not read until later. Publication of "Screen Memories" and *The Interpretation of Dreams* (dated, by editor, 1900).

1900   "Dora" analysis begun (October 14).

1901   Publication of *The Dream and Its Interpretation*, digest of *The Interpretation of Dreams*. Writes "Dreams and Hysteria," a report of Dora's analysis which will not be published until 1905, under another title. Relations with Fliess begin to deteriorate. Trip to Rome. Publication of *The Psychopathology of Everyday Life* (in periodical).

1902   Trip to Naples.

1903   First disciples (Federn, Stekel, etc.).

1904   Trip to Athens. Begins correspondence with Eugen Bleuler, in Zurich.

1905   Publication of *Three Essays on the Theory of Sexuality*, *Jokes and Their Relation to the Unconscious*, and "Fragment of an Analysis of a Case of Hysteria" (Dora).

1907   Visit from Jung (February). Meeting with Abraham. "Delusions and Dreams in Jensen's *Gradiva*" published.

1908   Visit from Sandor Ferenczi (February). Salzburg Congress (April). Second trip to England (September).

1909   Publication of "Analysis of a Phobia in a Five-Year-Old Boy" (little Hans) and "Notes upon a Case of Obsessional Neurosis" (the "Rat Man"). Trip to America (September) with Jung and Ferenczi. Lectures at Clark University (Worcester, Massachusetts).

1910   Nuremberg Congress. Foundation of International Society, with Jung as president. Publication of *Five Lectures on Psychoanalysis* (delivered in America) and *Leonardo da Vinci and a Memory of His Childhood*.

1911   Adler's resignation. Weimar Congress. Publication of study of the Schreber case under the title "Psychoanalytic Notes on an Autobiographical Account of a Case of Paranoia." From 1910 to 1912, several papers on technique published.

1913   Break with Jung. Munich Congress. Publication of *Totem and Taboo*.

1914   Publication of "The Moses of Michelangelo" and "On the History of the Psychoanalytical Movement." Jung's resignation.

1915   Composition of several essays on metapsychology.

1917   Publication of "Mourning and Melancholia" and *Introductory Lectures on Psycho-Analysis*.

1918   "From the History of an Infantile Neurosis" (the "Wolf Man") published.

1923   Diagnosis of cancer of the jaw. First operation. Publication of *The Ego and the Id*.

1925   Publication of *An Autobiographical Study* and "Negation." Death of Abraham in December.

1926   Publication of *The Question of Lay Analysis* and "Inhibition, Symptoms, and Anxiety."

1927   *The Future of an Illusion* published.

1929   *Civilization and Its Discontents* published.

1930   Receives Goethe prize (Anna takes his place at Frankfort and reads the speech of thanks he has written). September: death of Freud's mother. Collaboration with William C. Bullitt on writing *Thomas Woodrow Wilson*, which will not be published until 1967.

1932   *New Introductory Lectures on Psycho-Analysis* published.

1933   May: Nazis burn Freud's works in Berlin.

1937   "Analysis, Terminable and Interminable" published.

1938   March: Anschluss. Roosevelt and Mussolini intervene on Freud's behalf. He leaves for London in June. Treats patients almost until the end.

1939   September 23: death of Freud. Publication of the conclusion of *Moses and Monotheism*.

1940   Publication of *The Outline of Psychoanalysis* and "The Splitting of the Ego in the Process of Defence."

1950   *The Origins of Psychoanalysis* (letters to Fliess) first published (in German) in London.

1951   Death of Martha Freud. (She had kept all Freud's letters addressed to her. Only a very small number of them have been published.)

1954   *Original Notes* (on the analysis of the "Rat Man") published.

1967   Publication of *Thomas Woodrow Wilson* by Freud and Bullitt.

NOTES

Texts referred to most frequently:

The Complete Psychological Works of Sigmund Freud (Standard Edition), trans. under general editorship of James Strachey. London, Hogarth Press, 1953–1966 (distributed in the United States by The Macmillan Company). 24 vols. Cited as *Standard Edition*.

Freud, Sigmund, *The Origins of Psycho-Analysis. Letters to Wilhelm Fliess, Drafts and Notes, 1887–1902*, eds. Marie Bonaparte, Anna Freud, and Ernst Kris, trans. Eric Mosbacher and James Strachey. New York, Basic Books, 1954; London, Imago, 1954. Cited as *Origins*.

Jones, Ernest, *The Life and Work of Sigmund Freud*. New York, Basic Books, 1953–1955; London, Hogarth Press, 1953–1955 (under title *Sigmund Freud. Life and Work*). 3 vols. Cited as *Life of Freud*.

The Letters of Sigmund Freud, ed. Ernst L. Freud, trans. Tania and James Stern. New York, Basic Books, 1960; London, Hogarth Press, 1961.

A Psycho-Analytic Dialogue. The Letters of Sigmund Freud and Karl Abraham, 1907–1926, eds. Hilda C. Abraham and Ernst L. Freud, trans. Bernard Marsh and Hilda C. Abraham. New York, Basic Books, 1965; London, Hogarth Press, 1965. Cited as *Dialogue*.

Except in the case of the *Standard Edition*, references in the notes below are to the American editions of the foregoing books.

1. "Delusions and Dreams in Jensen's *Gradiva*" (1906), *Standard Edition*, Vol. IX, p. 7.

2. *Letters*, pp. 140–41.
3. *Ibid.*, p. 430.
4. *Origins*, p. 219.
5. "Screen Memories" (1899), *Standard Edition*, Vol. III, pp. 312–13.
6. *Ibid.*, p. 313.
7. "Some Reflections on Schoolboy Psychology" (1914), *Standard Edition*, Vol. XIII, pp. 241, 242.
8. *Letters*, p. 4.
9. *Ibid.*, p. 5.
10. *An Autobiographical Study* (1925), *Standard Edition*, Vol. XX, p. 8.
11. *Letters*, p. 111.
12. *Ibid.*, pp. 11–12.
13. *Ibid.*, pp. 101–2.
14. Quoted in Jones, *Life of Freud*, Vol. I, p. 176.
15. *Letters*, p. 60.
16. *Letters*, p. 185.
17. *Autobiographical Study*, *Standard Edition*, Vol. XX, p. 13.
18. "Charcot" (1893), *Standard Edition*, Vol. III, p. 20.
19. *Autobiographical Study*, *Standard Edition*, Vol. XX, p. 16.
20. *Ibid.*
21. "Five Lectures on Psycho-Analysis: First Lecture" (1910), *Standard Edition*, Vol. XI, p. 9.
22. *Letters*, p. 413.
23. *Origins*, p. 247.
24. *Studies on Hysteria* (with Breuer, 1895), *Standard Edition*, Vol. II, p. 123.
25. *Ibid.*, p. 300.
26. *Ibid.*, p. 223.
27. "A Short Account of Psycho-Analysis" (1924), *Standard Edition*, Vol. XIX, p. 194.
28. *Studies on Hysteria*, *Standard Edition*, Vol. II, pp. 160–61.
29. *Origins*, p. 134.
30. *Studies on Hysteria*, *Standard Edition*, Vol. II, p. 117, n. 1.
31. *An Outline of Psycho-Analysis* (1940), *Standard Edition*, Vol. XXIII, p. 177.
32. *The Psychopathology of Everyday Life* (1901), *Standard Edition*, Vol. VI, p. 250, n. 2. This passage omitted from 1907 edition and all subsequent editions.
33. *Origins*, pp. 202, 210–11.
34. *Ibid.*, p. 280.

35. *Ibid.*, pp. 305–6.
36. *Ibid.*, p. 212.
37. *Ibid.*, pp. 216–17.
38. *Ibid.*, p. 206.
39. *Ibid.*, pp. 223–24.
40. *Ibid.*, pp. 234–35.
41. *Ibid.*, p. 271.
42. *The Interpretation of Dreams* (1900), *Standard Edition*, Vol. IV, p. xxiii.
43. *Ibid.*, p. 277.
44. *Ibid.*, p. 598.
45. *Ibid.*, p. 137.
46. *Ibid.*, p. 138.
47. *Ibid.*
48. *Ibid.*, p. 139.
49. *Ibid.*, pp. 140–41.
50. *Ibid.*, p. 192.
51. *Ibid.*, p. 193.
52. *Ibid.*, p. 216.
53. *Ibid.*, p. xxv.
54. *Ibid.*, p. xxvi.
55. *The Psychopathology of Everyday Life*, *Standard Edition*, Vol. VI, p. 2.
56. *Ibid.*, pp. 2–3.
57. *Ibid.*, pp. 3–4.
58. *Ibid.*, p. 4.
59. "The Psychical Mechanism of Forgetfulness" (1898), *Standard Edition*, Vol. III, p. 295.
60. "Screen Memories," *Standard Edition*, Vol. III, pp. 308–9.
61. *Ibid.*, p. 311.
62. Jones, *Life of Freud*, Vol. I, p. 106.
63. *Psychopathology of Everyday Life*, *Standard Edition*, Vol. VI, pp. 253–54.
64. "Fragment of an Analysis of a Case of Hysteria" (case of Dora; 1905), *Standard Edition*, Vol. VII, p. 51.
65. *Ibid.*, p. 27, n. 1.
66. *Ibid.*, pp. 9–10.
67. *Autobiographical Study*, *Standard Edition*, Vol. XX, p. 38.
68. *Three Essays on the Theory of Sexuality* (1905), *Standard Edition*, Vol. VII, p. 133.
69. *Ibid.*, p. 178.
70. *Ibid.*, p. 239.

71. *Ibid.*, pp. 165, 167.

72. *Jokes and Their Relation to the Unconscious* (1905), *Standard Edition*, Vol. VIII, pp. 214–15.

73. *Autobiographical Study*, *Standard Edition*, Vol. XX, pp. 64–65.

74. *Letters*, p. 331.

75. "The Moses of Michelangelo" (1914), *Standard Edition*, Vol. XIII, p. 211.

76. *Dialogue*, p. 46.

77. "From the History of an Infantile Neurosis" (case of the "Wolf Man"; 1919), *Standard Edition*, Vol. XVII, p. 9.

78. Postscript to "Analysis of a Phobia in a Five-Year-Old Boy" (case of little Hans; 1909), *Standard Edition*, Vol. X, p. 148.

79. "From the History of an Infantile Neurosis" ("Wolf Man"), *Standard Edition*, Vol. XVII, p. 53.

80. Jones, *Life of Freud*, Vol. II, p. 83.

81. "Psycho-Analytic Notes on an Autobiographical Account of a Case of Paranoia (Dementia Paranoides)" (case of Schreber; 1911), *Standard Edition*, Vol. XII, pp. 55–56.

82. *Letters*, p. 50.

83. *Origins*, p. 237.

84. "Formulations on the Two Principles of Mental Functioning" (1911), *Standard Edition*, Vol. XII, p. 225.

85. "On Narcissism: An Introduction" (1914), *Standard Edition*, Vol. XIV, p. 91.

86. *Ibid.*, p. 101.

87. "The Unconscious" (1915), *Standard Edition*, Vol. XIV, p. 188.

88. Quoted in Jones, *Life of Freud*, Vol. II, p. 329.

89. *Letters*, p. 259.

90. *The Ego and the Id* (1923), *Standard Edition*, Vol. XIX, p. 56.

91. Postscript to *Autobiographical Study*, *Standard Edition*, Vol. XX, p. 72.

92. *Autobiographical Study*, *Standard Edition*, Vol. XX, p. 59.

93. "The Claims of Psycho-Analysis to Scientific Interest" (1913), *Standard Edition*, Vol. XIII, pp. 186–87.

94. *The Future of an Illusion* (1928), *Standard Edition*, Vol. XXI, p. 35.

95. *Ibid.*, p. 48.

96. "Letter to the Editor of the Jewish Press Centre in Zurich" (1925), *Standard Edition*, Vol. XIX, p. 291.

97. *Autobiographical Study, Standard Edition*, Vol. XX, p. 9.
98. Jones, *Life of Freud*, Vol. I, p. 348.
99. Heinz Hartmann, *Ego Psychology and the Problem of Adaptation*, trans. David Rapaport (New York, International Universities Press, 1964), p. 6.
100. *Standard Edition*, Vol. XXI, p. 255.

INDEX